I0021429

Writing for Busy Bloggers
How to Write Blog Posts That are Easy to Read

The Busy Blogger Series
Book 1

By: Brian Forbes

ISBN# 9781652626329

Dedication

For my Mother, who is the reason that I am so talkative.

I Love You Mom.

Introduction

The following is a no fluff collection of actionable strategies that you can use to format your blog posts so they are easy to read.

This isn't about pretty pictures or charts. It's about showing you what you can do right now to make your posts look the best they possibly can.

Easier to read blog posts means your readers will stay longer, consume more of your great content, and start building trust with your site.

Most of your readers aren't really readers. They are skimmers. These formatting tips will help you create beautiful looking blog posts that are easy to skim, but also satisfy the readers that like to devour every word.

There are simple things you can do as a beginner to structure your posts so they are clear, organized, helpful, and present the best answer to the question you are solving.

These are not difficult or hard to implement, and you can quickly tweak a post to fit the better formatting in a few minutes. Once you get comfortable with the process, you will naturally write all of your posts with the same level of organization and structure.

If you look at the best sites out these, they are doing one thing really well. They all make it very easy for their readers to find what they are looking for.

That will be a recurring theme throughout the book,

because in the end the best thing you can do for your blog is make it easy for your readers to consume your content. Keep that in mind as you read, and you will be well on your way to creating blog posts that your readers will love.

Happy Writing.

How to Use This Book

Writing for Busy Bloggers is broken up into several chapters, each one aimed at a specific area of your post. Though you can read the book from start to finish and be very successful at absorbing the strategies, you can also jump around if you like.

I recommend that you start by reading chapter one, because these are the big ideas that you can use to make decisions about your site. Even if you don't find a specific answer to a question you may have, you can run the questions through some of these big filters and find your answer. These pillars represent the overall goals of a well formatted blog post, and they can solve a lot of beginner questions.

After that, go to the sections that you need the most, and read the others last.

Finally, if you are a beginner, then read the book in order, because the ideas will build upon one another and help you learn faster.

The goal is to write the clearest, most understandable post possible, and even though it sounds simple, there are a lot of things that go into it. Read the book in order, and start using the strategies to make your blog posts look amazing.

Table Of Contents

Chapter One – Big Ideas and Concepts
These are the Main Ideas that will help you make the best decisions for the formatting of your posts.

Chapter Two – Typography and Writing
Things you can do with font, typeface and size to make your post easier to read and understand.

Chapter Three – Post Layout and Elements
The perfect post layout to organize and present your content in an easy to consume way.

Chapter Four – Design and Navigation

Creating a beautiful site that doesn't distract your readers, and doesn't slow down your site.

Chapter Five – Calls to Action and Links

Creating and placing calls to action and making them the most effective on your site.

Chapter Six – Headers and Footers

Best practices for headers and footers so they contribute to your overall blog post.

Chapter Severn – Sidebars and Widgets

How to use sidebars and widgets and how they have changed with the way sites are viewed now.

Chapter Eight – Evaluating the Post

The best ways to edit your posts for content as well as grammar and spelling mistakes to ensure an interruption free reading experience.

Chapter One

Big Ideas and Concepts

Make Your Post Easy to Read

The most important thing that you can do when writing your blog posts is to make sure that they are easy to read. This is the one rule that guides all the rest.

When a reader finally clicks on your post, and they decide to consume the content, it's very important that the process is easy, and that they can find the information they're looking for without having to struggle.

If you focus on this one aspect of blogging, you can do really well at providing an experience that will keep your readers coming back.

Essentially what you are doing is writing a blog post for people that don't like to read blog posts. I know it sounds funny, but that's really the truth.

"The majority of people that encounter your site will do nothing but skim the headings and briefly look for the information that they came for."

The majority of people that encounter your site will do nothing but skim the headings and briefly look for the information that they came for. It's strange that people that don't like to read search written content for their answers, but that's the way it works.

If you want to create blog posts that do well in search rankings, you need to write for the average reader, and they just don't like to read very much. However, this is actually not very difficult to do, and at the same time you're doing it you can also satisfy the people that enjoy reading.

All of the post formatting ideas that are coming up will show you exactly what you need to do to make your post as easy-to-read as possible. These will keep your readers on your post longer, and help send the right signals to the search engines that you are creating the type of material that people are looking for.

You Have 3 Seconds

Unfortunately, people that land on your site or only going to dwell for about three seconds before they decide whether all your hard work is worth reading or not. Your book is going to be judged by its cover

over and over again.

We live in a world where so much information is available, and the speed at which that information can be delivered is so outstanding that we've all been conditioned to expect instant results. When it comes to your blog, and your posts, you need to think about that when you do your formatting.

"There are a lot of different things that you can do to captivate your reader within the first few seconds."

There are a lot of different things that you can do to captivate your reader within the first few seconds. These include opening really big, and showing them exactly why they need to stay.

They also include giving the information right away, creating an attractive look to your site, and avoiding any of the major turnoffs that scare readers away. In the end, the first three seconds and your above the fold content are going to be what helps the reader make the decision to stay or leave.

When you are evaluating your blog post, pay attention to the part that you see as soon as the post loads. This is called the above the fold content, which is an old newspaper term for the part of the paper that you can see face up on the newsstand. This is the part that you can see with no effort, and it needs to be outstanding. (more on this coming up)

People in general don't like putting in a lot of effort for the results, so even something as simple as asking them to scroll down through your post to find the information they're looking for is problematic.

It's much better to open strongly, and make sure that there is no misunderstanding that it's worth sticking around and reading the post.

Most of the tips that are coming up are going to help reinforce the importance of the first few seconds when the reader decides if hours and hours of your hard work are worth their time. If you incorporate many of these techniques into your post formatting, you give yourself the best chance to keep the largest number of readers possible.

Write a Great Headline

Your headline is the most important part of your blog post. It is more important than the content, more important than the images, and more important than any other element that you create.

The reason? If nobody likes your headline, they will never read your post.

"Your headline is the most important part of your blog post."

Such is the truth in a world full of quick information and easy answers. If your headline isn't good enough to make them interested in your content, they will never read what you have to say.

If you think about it, the majority of times that people interact with your website it will first interact with one of your headlines. This may be through organic search traffic, or it may be through seeing a link in social media.

The part of your website that they see is a title, and sometimes they may see a very short description as well. However, that title is going to be the only thing that they read, and the only thing that they use to make a decision on whether to click through and read your post.

This makes the title extraordinarily important, because you could have the best answer in the world for your particular keyword, but if the title is awful, nobody will ever know how amazing your post really is.

Knowing this information, all you need to do is spend some time learning how to write amazing titles that captivate the reader's attention and hook them into reading your post.

This is a little easier said than done, and crafting good titles does require a little bit of effort. However, all you need to do is frequently surround yourself with well-written titles and do a little practice, and you'll develop the skill pretty quickly.

One of the places that I recommend you begin immediately is on popular websites that receive a lot of traffic in your niche. Start there to get a good idea of at least what's expected of people that come to a website similar to yours.

After that, check out one of the best websites on the Internet when it comes to writing titles, and that's called BuzzFeed. This is a website is geared toward younger readers, so many of the articles may sound childish to you, but that's their target audience.

If you look past the words, and look at the way they are written, and the phrasing, you'll see a brilliance in title construction that has been a key to their success.

The point of a title is to get you to click on the link. Read that again. The point of the title, and the only point of the title is to get the reader to take the next step, which is to click.

If you evaluate all of your titles from that perspective, and only that perspective, you'll have a much better time creating clickable headlines.

This means you need to put the information about the post into the title, but you also need to do it in a

"The point of a title is to get you to click on the link."

way that entices people to want more. There are a lot of different ways to do that, and entire books have been written about crafting headlines and drawing readers into your world.

I recommend that you do a simple Google search for how to write blog posts headlines. Read a couple of articles and use the tips they share to write better headlines for yourself.

Most of the content that's out there about writing headlines is pretty similar. It's a bit of an art, but it's definitely something you can master once you start thinking about your headlines the right way.

Once you have the basic structure in place, I recommend that you write 10 good headlines for every one of your blog posts, and then pick the one that makes the most sense in the end. This will give you a lot of reps in the beginning, and will help you develop your headline writing muscle.

Once you do this for maybe 50 or 100 posts, or whenever you feel comfortable, you can back off to maybe only writing a few headlines for each one, because you'll be much better at going straight to the best one after you've had about your practice.

Make headline creation a huge part of your process, and the more time you spend crafting the perfect phrase, the more people you will get to click and read your post.

Above the Fold Content

Above the fold content is the first impression that your readers have when they look at your website. It's everything that loads immediately on their screen before they take any action, or scroll down.

This is a very common term that you'll hear as a blogger, because it's an

"Above the fold content is the first impression that your readers have when they look at your website."

important thing to know. The first impression you have on your readers is extremely important, so investing a little time in your above the fold area is definitely worth it.

Going back to the few seconds that you have to capture your reader, it just makes sense that you're above the fold content is outstanding, and captivating. There are a lot of different ways that you can do this, and if you do it right, you'll convert the maximum amount of opportunities into readers.

One way to do this is with images, and since people are visual beings, a captivating image can hold your attention for quite a while, and get you used to staying on the webpage. You can also do this with a promise, or a few simple words to tell them exactly why they need to stay on your site.

For each blogger, the above the fold content is going to be different, and that's okay.

You may like to open with impressive pictures, or you may like to open with your title, and a subtitle that reinforces the importance of the post.

However you do it, and there are several ideas coming up, it's important that this area be effective.

After all, you're going to spend quite a long time crafting and developing each one of your posts. It would be a complete shame and a tragedy on the highest level to have a poor interaction right at the beginning, and cause your readers to run away.

Even if you have the best answer, and the best post, people just aren't going to stick around if you scare them off from the beginning. So, after you're done formatting your amazing post, take a look at the way that it loads on different devices.

On each one, assess whether the above the fold section is doing its job in the best way possible.

If it is, then you're done.

If it's not, think about how you can improve that section. Most of the time, it's not much more

"Even if you have the best answer, and the best post, people just aren't going to stick around if you scare them off from the beginning"

difficult than just rearranging a few elements on the page.

Once you do that, the top area of your page will become much more effective, and it will look better too. In most cases, this is really a quick fix, but it will make a big difference in getting your reader to go to the next step.

Open With a Promise

One of the easiest ways to help your readers understand the importance of sticking around and reading the rest of your post is to just make a promise right in the beginning. This is a short, sweet little promise that tells them exactly why they need to stay.

"Just start by telling them exactly what you plan on telling them."

Instead of beating around the bush, or writing some long winded and drawn out introduction, just start by telling them exactly what you plan on telling them. Give them the reason right in the beginning, and don't mince any words about.

If your blog post is about how to make the world's best chicken salad, tell them right in the introduction that by the end of this post they will know how to make the world's best chicken salad. There is absolutely no reason to deny them that information, and you are doing yourself a disservice by hiding the ultimate goal of your post from your readers.

After all, it's no surprise for them. They came to your site by searching for how to make an awesome chicken salad. When you tell them that's exactly what you're going to teach them, they already know.

It's very common in introductions to do a quick preview on what your document is about. On websites it's no different. The only real difference is how much time you have.

When people sit down to read something on paper, they tend to consume a lot more of it than online. Again, it has to do with how fast information can be transferred back and forth, and people are just used to a faster experience on a device.

That being said, the major difference that you have

to account for when you're making a promise in your introduction for your post is to just spit it out a little faster.

Don't wait until you are three sentences into your post before you tell them exactly why they should be here. Instead, use your first two sentences to make your promise.

Getting people to read two sentences can sometimes be a stretch, and I know it sounds crazy but people just don't like to read anymore. Use those first two sentences to tell people exactly what they came for, and it will do two things.

"Don't wait until you are three sentences into your post before you tell them exactly why they should be here."

First, the people that accidentally landed on your website for a different reason will know that it's not for them, and they'll leave. This is actually a good thing, because you don't want your name associated with bad answers.

Even if your answers are all very good, if it's not what they're looking for, you can create the perception that they are bad.

Second, the people that are looking for exactly what your post is all about will be really excited, because searching online can actually be a little bit of a stressful process.

When you relieve that tension immediately, it makes it a lot easier for them to decide to continue reading. That's really what it's all about, there's a little bit of tension whenever someone lands on a new webpage.

Think about when you do a search yourself. You land on someone's page, you have no idea who they are, but you're hoping that the right answer exists somewhere on that page. The whole time you're looking, you're weighing in your mind whether it's worth it to continue.

The longer it takes for you to prove to yourself that

this is the right destination, the more likely you are to hit the back button and go select another result.

After all, why would you waste time reading an article about something that's not to do with the answer you're looking for? You wouldn't, so whether it's in the front of your mind or not, you are always slightly worried when you start to read a post.

Instead of allowing your readers to be worried, and weigh in their mind with every passing second whether they should leave your site, just tell them exactly what they need to know right in the beginning, and you will instantly extinguish all of that tension.

This will also do a third thing, which is only possible when you accomplish the second thing. The third thing is that those readers will actually stick around a lot longer, because you boosted their confidence in what they're reading.

The weighing process is still happening, but it's a lot

more forgiving and understanding now that they know you promised to tell them what they're looking for.

This third thing is really only the very first small step in a much *"Trust is an amazing thing, because it can get people to stick with you."* bigger concept, and that's building trust with your audience.

Trust is an amazing thing, because it can get people to stick with you even through troubled and difficult times because they know you're reliable.

Starting people off on the right foot and making a promise, then ultimately keeping that promise is one of the very first small things that you can do to begin building trust with your audience.

It's going to take a very long time of course, and you'll have to have several good experiences with each one of your readers in order to start developing that trust, but there's absolutely no reason not to get started right away.

Open big with a promise, and do it within the first two lines. You'll immediately disarm a good portion of your readers defense structure, and you'll help put them at ease while they search your post more confidently looking for what they came for.

After that, all you need to do is deliver the goods.

Help the Reader Build Momentum

Another big idea to pay attention to when you're writing your blog posts is that you want to use different techniques in order to help the reader build momentum. Again, people don't like to read, but if you make them think that they're doing really well, and flying through the content, they will keep reading longer than you might expect.

Since nobody really likes to read, you need to use little tricks to make your readers think they're doing well. In reality, tricks might not be the best word, because there's no evil side to it, is just writing and structuring your post in a way that makes it easy to keep moving without interruption.

This can be as simple as using shorter sentences, bulleted lists, smaller words, and more space in

"People don't like to read, but if you make them think that they're doing really well, they will keep reading longer than you might expect."

between the lines. All of these things help your reader have an easier time consuming your content, and that helps them build momentum.

The momentum that they build is psychologically pleasing to them, and it makes them feel like they are are reading really well and that the process is easy.

When the process is easy, they don't feel the urge to

stop reading, so they continue, and the momentum is reinforced yet again.

You can use this big idea as a way to make decisions when you run into something that you don't have a specific rule for. In this way, these big guidelines can help you figure out different aspects of your blog post that you haven't even thought about yet.

"Big guidelines can help you figure out things about your blog that you don't have specific rules for."

For example, if you're entertaining the idea of putting a huge blinking call to action with a long video in your header, but you haven't specifically read anything about the success or failure of that particular method, you can use the momentum idea to make the decision.

Does it sound like a huge blinking image with a long video right in the beginning of your blog post is the best way to help your reader build momentum? No, that doesn't sound like it will help them build momentum at all.

So, even though you may not have studied anything about this particular element of a blog post, you'll know that is probably good idea to skip.

Make Your Posts Easy to Skim

The majority of readers who come to your site are just going to skim the content and look for the information they need. This means the majority of your writing isn't even going to be read by the larger number of people that come to the site.

Knowing this, you can do a lot of different things to make your post easy to skim, so that we the reader can get what they came for, and continue on with their day.

It would be nice to think that you can keep people on your site forever, but it's much better to just give them what they're looking for and let them keep going.

The problem with hiding the information is that most people are not going to put in the effort to find it. When they leave your site and go pick a different search result, it sends a signal to the search engines that you didn't provide the answer that you were supposed to. If this happens enough times, the search engines will stop returning your post for that particular search term.

"The problem with hiding information is that most people are not going to put in any effort to look for it."

The amount of time a reader spends reading your post is also a signal to the search engines as to the quality of the content. However, don't think that because you give them the answer right away and they may not spend as much time, that the search engines are going to frown upon you.

They're not, because when you give people the right answers, there next actions provide the signal to the search engines that your content was the one that solved the question or the problem that they had.

This is a good thing, because it helps the search engines trust your post as being the best, or one of the best results for the particular search.

Again, the more you can do to help your reader be able to skim your content and find what they're looking for, the better. These include things like making short sections, using headings often, and not burying the goods at the bottom of the post.

Make the Information Easy to Find

On top of making your post easy to skim, it's also really important to make it easy to find the information that the reader came for. People have very short attention spans, so if it's not easy to find the answer, even if it's there, most readers are going to back out and click on another search result to solve the problem.

This is a poor signal to the search engines about the quality of your writing, and the quality of the answer provided for the search term.

Instead of withholding the answer until the very end, or hiding it behind several different links that force your readers to take action when they don't even know you, just give the answer that you promised to give.

Now, you don't need to put the answer at the very top of the post and let the readers know that they don't have to read anything more, but you do have to present it in a way that makes it easy to find.

One of the things it's absolutely infuriating to a lot of readers is when they have to scroll all the way to the bottom of the post in order to find what they're looking for. This is very common with recipe and food bloggers, because they bury the recipe card at the bottom.

I totally understand why this is done, because they get more ad impressions and make more money that way, but it does drive people nuts to have to dig deep. In fact, if it takes too long to load, the readers will leave, and eventually that post wont show up in the search results anymore.

This is a perfect example of a short-term strategy that doesn't have the long term in mind. The reason that the recipe cards are at

"If a post takes too long to load and the reader can't find the answer, they will leave.."

the bottom is so that you have to scroll past all of the ads that pop up in the post, and the blogger gets paid for every one of them that you see.

So, the logic is that by making you scroll all the way to the bottom, you're guaranteed to see the ads before you get your recipe and leave.

The long-term problem with this strategy is that unless the site loads incredibly fast, and scrolling to the bottom isn't a burden for the reader, they are just going to hit the back button after they become frustrated and then go pick another search result.

This is where the short-term idea of getting revenue on the ads by forcing people to scroll becomes a long-term problem because eventually search engines will stop returning your post because people continuously leave it and search for their answer elsewhere.

"Everything that you tell your reader becomes a promise in their minds."

Even if the answer you gave was really good, if nobody actually gets it, then it's no better than a bad answer.

All that being said, make sure that you allow your readers to find the answer easily and naturally without any barriers in between.

This will make your readers happier, and it can also encourage them to build trust in you, your site, and your ability to provide the answers that are looking for.

Keep Your Promise

When you make a promise to your reader, you need to keep your promise. In reality, everything that you tell your reader becomes a promise in their minds. So unless you plan on delivering, don't tell them you are.

I always recommend opening your blog posts with a short promise that tells the reader exactly what they are going to get by sticking around. This is how you make it easier for them to continue reading your content, knowing that they're going to get what they came for.

This is a huge technique for getting people to stick

around on your post when most people hit the back button within a few seconds. So, if you make a promise, and you start to create that trust, you need to make sure that you don't violate that trust.

The easiest way to do this is to simply provide exactly what you said you were going to provide.

If your opening line says that you're going to teach five different ways of removing a beer bottle cap without a bottle opener, then your post better have five unique, different ways of removing a beer bottle cap without a bottle opener.

"If you make a promise, and you start to create that trust, you need to make sure that you don't violate that trust."

This sounds very obvious, but you'd be surprised how many blog posts fail to deliver what they say they are going to deliver. Again, it may be some way of trying to game the search algorithm and get more results in the short run, but over time the algorithm will patch itself and this strategy will no longer work.

In the end, delivering what you say you are going to deliver is the best way to please your readers, and in turn send the right signals to the search engines that your content is a good quality.

When you don't keep your promise, this is typically called click bait, or bait and switch. You've probably seen something like this before, especially when it comes to the cover slides on videos.

Appealing to the baser instincts, sometimes bloggers will use a picture that draws your attention but has absolutely nothing to do with the video. You don't know that of course, you just click on the video in hopes to see more, and you end up watching some video that's totally unrelated.

In the end, you feel cheated, and it gives you a really bad taste about that particular site, and videos from that particular maker. In the short run they got what they wanted, because you watched the video.

However, in the long run they're never going to come back, so eventually the strategy is just not going to work.

Don't bait and switch, and don't use click bait on your content that has nothing to do with what your content is about. All you will do in a case like this is upset your readers, and though you will get a short term bump, it will not last.

Increase Dwell Time

For the same reason that you don't want people to run away from your website, you also want to do little things to keep them there longer.

The amount of time that someone spends on your site is called dwell time, and it's an indicator to the search engines that people are getting what they're looking for. It's also an indication that you aren't using click bait to get people onto your post, and then disappointing them by not delivering the goods.

The amount of time that someone spends on your post is important, because it makes logical sense that if people are spending more time consuming your content, they are doing so of their own free will, and because they enjoy it, or need it.

This is a strong signal, because what people choose to do is something that you can't directly influence through unethical practices.

"The amount of time that someone spends on your post is important."

Though the last part is up for debate, most of the practices that artificially inflate dwell time have been figured out by the search engines and those techniques no longer work.

However, there are a lot of different things that you can do to help people stick around, but in a way that is positive and beneficial to them. One of the best is adding video content to your posts.

When most bloggers think about blogging, they tend to think about written words.

While that's the majority of blog content, adding video is a great way to keep your readers on your site longer, but also provide some additional content that is useful to them.

Even if you were to only record a five-minute video of you talking about the post, explaining what they will learn, and even providing some additional insights that aren't in the text, you can significantly increase the amount of time that the user spends on the page.

Again, this is a tremendous signal to the search engines that people are liking what you are providing.

Video content is actually pretty easy to produce, and you more than likely already have a very good video recorder in your pocket. Your phone records better video than most handheld camcorders, especially those from a few years ago. Don't let the fact that it's a phone fool you, it's one of the most powerful devices that you have at your disposal.

There are also tons of free video editing software packages that are available online, and there

"Video content is actually pretty easy to produce, and you more than likely already have a very good video recorder in your pocket."

are also several that come built into different computers, depending on which one you bought. There are even paid software options, but in most cases you don't even have to go that route.

All you need to do is record a nice video of yourself against a solid background, which could be a wall in your home, office, or shop, and just talk about the post for a few minutes.

After you have this video completed, you can upload it to YouTube, and then embed it in your post so that way you don't have to store the videos on your own server.

It will also be in a format that's very familiar to people, because the YouTube video box is the standard in the industry, and basically everyone knows how to use it.

Place the video inside of your post in a section that makes the most sense, and highlight the video with its own heading and a brief description that gets people to play the video. You should think of this as a mini headline, because the point of this particular piece of text is to get them to click on the video.

If nobody clicks on the video, nobody watches the video, so just like the headline is more important than your blog post, this particular section of text is more important than your video.

Another thing that you can do to increase the

amount of time that people spend on your site without manipulating them, and in a positive way is to include good visuals.

People love to see pictures, so if you give them something to look at, they will spend time looking at it.

This isn't just limited to pictures though, because you can do graphics that have text on them, such as quotes, or powerful statements. All of these things break up the text, and give the readers something to stare at for a few seconds.

"People love to see pictures, so if you give them something to look at, they will spend time looking at it."

If you have a very long post that has several outstanding images or graphics, it can add a few seconds for each one of them, and throughout the entire post that can add up to quite a significant additional amount of time.

Finally, infographics are all the rage right now, and for good reason.

People just like information arranged in a nice-looking way, with pictures. In a way, were all just kids looking for an easy way, and a fun way to consume the information.

You can create infographics yourself, or you can pay to have been created by somebody else.

Either way you go, adding a nice infographics that are visually appealing, entertaining, and full of great information can significantly increase the amount of time that someone spends on the site.

Inspect Every Element

An easy filter to put your decisions through is to think about whether or not it makes the post easier to read.

You should inspect every single element on your page, and ask that one simple question. Does it make the post easier to read? If the answer is yes, then leave it. If the answer is no, then it's a good idea to look at that particular element and see what you can do to either improve it so it makes the post easier to read, or remove it entirely.

This is a really easy way to make decisions when it comes to the different elements of your blog post. If it makes the post easier to read, and contributes positively to the reader experience, then leave it in place. If it doesn't, see if there is a way to rework that element into something that does.

"You should inspect every single element on your page, and ask that one simple question. Does it make the post easier to read?"

There are going to be times when you just have to eliminate things from your blog posts, even though you might really like them yourself. That's okay, and the quicker you break up with your blog post, the easier it's going to be to do what needs to be done based on logic and sound reasoning.

You love your blog, but your readers don't, especially the new ones. You may have some folks who do fall in love with your blog over time, but in order to get to that point, you need to get past their initial bad habits as a new reader.

"You love your blog, but your readers don't, especially the new ones."

The way that you do that is to make sure all of your elements make sense, and that they all contribute to making the post easy to read, and easy for the user to get exactly the information that they were searching for.

Do this one thing right, and in the long term it will help you create and retain the largest number of readers.

Even people that have been with you for years will appreciate the fact that you have such an easy reading style, and that you don't hide your information.

They will grow accustomed to your particular way of presenting the content, and it will become an expectation.

As you make decisions on the different pieces that go into your website, don't ever lose sight of the fact that you are training your readers have a certain set of expectations.

If you train them well, they will start to rely on you. When they start to rely on you, that's when you start to get readers coming directly to you to search for the answers instead of going elsewhere.

Break up with your blog as soon as possible, and don't make emotional decisions when it comes to what you keep and what you don't. It all comes down to the user experience, and making it as easy as possible for them to read your post.

Let Your Readers Know You

Finally, it's important that you let your readers get to know you, because people form relationships with other people.

You don't need to tell everyone on your site your life story, but it's okay to let them know how you feel, especially when it comes to content that requires an opinion.

It pretty much doesn't matter what type of blog you have, there are always opportunities to make it personal, and help your readers like you.

Think about it. You just behave differently around people you like than around strangers. This manifests itself in a number of different ways, but the way that is the most significant to bloggers is in the trust factor.

When somebody likes you, they start to trust you, and they will behave differently.

The new behavior that you're looking for is for them to come directly to you for the answers, and to spend more time on your site because they are comfortable and they trust you.

One of the best ways to get people to like you is to first get them to know you. After all, can't like somebody that you don't know.

One simple way of doing this is to just have a picture of you somewhere that is prominent on the site. This lets your readers see what you

"One of the best ways to get people to like you is to first get them to know you. After all, they can't like you if they don't know you, so that's the first step."

look like, and help them associate your face with your writing.

You can also incorporate your face or pictures of you doing things as part of your content. This way, the two become almost inseparable, or indistinguishable.

When people start to associate you with your content, the trust factor goes up significantly, and your readers start showing up for you, almost regardless of what you are publishing.

Whether you are aware of it or not, you tend to give a lot of brakes to the people that you like and trust where as you don't give nearly as many to people that you don't know.

"Whether you are aware of it or not, you tend to give a lot of brakes to the people that you like and trust where as you don't give nearly as many to people that you don't know."

There's nothing wrong with this behavior course, and it's something that helps keep you safe in the real world, but it's also something that you can use as a writer to influence your readers in a positive way.

Think about your favorite band, or your favorite actor.

You'll follow them from album to album or movie to movie and you pretty much always have a good time. Some are better than others of course, but in general you like pretty much everything they do.

In contrast, someone who doesn't like that band or that actor as much, they will say negative things about an album or movie that comes out that just isn't quite as good as what they were used to.

For them, it's about the content, not about the person. For you on the other hand, it's all about the person, and because you like them, they get a break.

This is a huge benefit for that actor or musician, because they build a little bit of a relationship with you, and it means that you'll still show up for them, even though their content may not always be as awesome as you remember it.

It's okay though, because you like them, and for you, the content is always good.

It's important that you don't misinterpret what you just read. This doesn't mean you can form a good relationship with your readers and then start producing crappy content. That's definitely not the big takeaway from this section.

What it means is that if a particular piece of content doesn't resonate one hundred percent with one of your readers that trusts you, they won't leave you forever because of it.

What it means is that they will be more forgiving, and they will keep coming back because they know that you'll be posting some awesome stuff that speaks more to them eventually.

They also know that not everything is going to ring their bell every time.

Instead of running away because they don't know you, they will stick around because they trust you.

Another way to let your readers get to know you is

to not be afraid to say how you feel in your post.

Remember, you are in competition against millions of other posts that explain the exact same thing that you are trying to explain. In a case like this, it's better to be different, and the only way to be different is to be yourself.

There is only one you in this world, and as cliché as that sounds, it's your go to card for being unique.

"Remember, you are in competition against millions of other posts that explain the exact same thing that you are trying to explain."

Nobody else can do it just like you, and you don't have to fake it at all to get it right.

This is as simple as saying how you feel when it comes down to it, and not writing long-winded sentences that check off all the boxes so everyone is happy.

It's about just saying that something is a certain way

without saying that it's only a certain way in certain instances at certain times and for certain people. This is absolutely the worst way to blog, because it takes you completely out of it.

"People that love you will do anything for you."

Again, it's much better to have an opinion than have no opinion. It's also much better to be loved by a few than to have a lukewarm or indifferent response by millions. People that love you will do anything for you. They will show up, they will read, and they will buy.

People that only like you, or are indifferent to you will never stick around, because there's no reason.

You are no different than anyone else, and there's nothing unique about your content that can't be found on 1000 other websites.

You definitely don't have to go over the top when it comes to your opinions and develop a character for yourself. What you do need to incorporate is as much you as possible.

Whenever you go through your reading and you catch yourself hedging your bets, or writing a really complicated statement in an effort to try to appeal to everyone, you're going to end up appealing to no one.

Instead of doing that, just write how you feel, and do it in a way that is non-confrontational or threatening.

Not only will this particular style of writing resonate more with your readers, and help them get to know you better, it will also feel more natural to you, so the process will be easier.

It actually feels a lot more like faking it when you try to appeal to everyone. Don't waste your time, and just be yourself.

Tips and Tricks for Big Ideas

Here are a few tips and tricks that can help you get the most out of these big ideas for blogging:

- Use the big ideas as a filter to help you make your decisions.

- If you don't have a specific rule for something, think back to the big ideas and it will help you make the right decision.

- It's better to make a few people love you than to have millions of people indifferent to you.

- You only have a little bit of time to get people to read your post, so tell them exactly why they should stay right in the beginning.

- With everything that you write, and every element on your post, help the reader build momentum and find the information they came for.

- Keep all of your promises, and give your readers additional content to help them stay on your page longer, and get more benefit from finding your site.

- Help your readers trust you by giving them what they came for, and solving the problem.

- Readers that trust you will stick with you much longer than readers who don't know you, or can't see a difference between your site and the millions of others on the Internet.

- You are unique, so the easiest way to make your posts unique is to allow your own personality to shine through.

Chapter Two

Typography and Writing

When it comes to creating blog posts, the typography and writing, meaning the words themselves and the way the words look have a huge impact on your reader. If the way the writing looks on the page is inviting, and appears easy to consume, your reader will stay longer on your page.

They will get the information that they're looking for, and they will be happier for it.

However, if the words are difficult to read, the grammar is awful, and the font is very small, you'll create a negative experience that drives readers away.

Depending on how extreme the typographical issues are on your website, you might drive people away instantly, the moment your site loads.

"Investing time in how the words look on the page can help you send the right signals."

This is an awful signal to send, and in cases like this it only takes a very short amount of time for your traffic to completely disappear.

If you are brand-new blogger, investing time in how the words look on the page can help you send the right signals to increase your traffic when you do have people land.

This is the ultimate goal, because when you make things easier for your readers, they send the right signals to the search engines for you, and that turns into even more readers.

There are a lot of different ways for you to address the way that the words look in your post, and each one of these will help your posts look better, and encourage your readers to spend more time reading and consuming your awesome content.

Use a Larger Font Size

One of the first things that you can do as a new blogger, or even as an experienced blogger who hasn't addressed this particular area of their site is to use a larger font size. Most web material is consumed on cell phones and tablets, so the screens are very small.

If you use larger text, you make it easier for your

readers to consume the material, and they will stick around longer because of it.

Most websites default at around a 12 point font, which may look fine when you're building your website on your computer, but it's going to look incredibly tiny when you finally look at that blog post on your phone.

Again, since most people are going to interact with your site on their phones, that's really

"A 12 point font on a desktop is going to look much easier to read than a 12 point font on a cell phone."

where you need to look in order to evaluate how easy or difficult it is to read your text.

Instead of using the same old 12 point font as everyone else, consider going to anywhere between 18 and 20 points for your font.

Initially, this will seem extraordinarily large and

scary. However, once you see the way that it resolves on mobile, you'll feel like your website is so much easier to read and consume. Your readers will feel the same way, and bigger text is definitely a good thing.

After you adjust the size of your body text, you may need to go back through and take a look at the size of your headers.

Most of those are based off of the size of the body text, so if you significantly increase the size of the body text, it may blunt the effectiveness of your headers a little bit, because they don't quite look as large and bold in contrast anymore.

This is a fairly easy process with most themes, especially ones that are paid.

All you have to do is go into the typography section and adjust the sizes of at least headings 1, 2 and 3 proportionately to the amount that you increased the body font.

Just play around with it a little bit, and make sure that you can see a distinguishable size difference between your body text, and each of your three most used headings.

Increasing the size of the words on the page also does another thing besides just making them easier to read without needing a microscope. Since the letters are bigger, less of them fit on a line, so your website will render more lines.

"Faster reading and scrolling keeps your reader engaged, because they feel like they are making good progress."

The more lines you render, more the reader will have to scroll to continue reading. This is great, because it sends a signal to the reader that they're making a lot of progress, because their scrolling down like crazy.

This positive signal keeps your reader engaged, because they feel like they are making good progress. It will keep them going longer, and all because you increased the size of the letters.

One of the easiest ways to test this process is to just create a draft page in WordPress, and then insert some text for each of the three headings as well as some body text.

Then, preview it in your browser to see what it looks like. If you like the way that it looks on a computer, publish the page and take a quick look at how it appears on mobile.

"When you have a font size that is easier to read, it will help you keep readers on your site longer."

The nice thing about doing this process with a page instead of a post is that nobody's going to see the page, because it won't appear anywhere on your site unless you create a menu location for it.

This lets you check out the page and see if you like the sizes without having to show the world that you are messing around with your site.

If there is anything left to be desired about the way that your heading one, heading two, heading three, and paragraph text interact, make those changes in your theme settings and preview that page again.

Make sure that you check on desktop and mobile, and if you have one, check on a tablet as well. Once you are satisfied that the headings look good, and are proportional to each other, you are done with this part of the process.

Now, you'll have a font size that is easier to read, and it will help you keep readers on your site longer.

Easy to Read Typefaces

Once your font size is easy to read on all devices, the next thing you need to turn your attention to is the typeface. This is the thing that people often confuse with a font. The font is the size, the typeface is what it looks like.

For example, right now you're reading a Georgia typeface, with a font size of 14 points. This is an excellent font for books, because it's easy to read, and it has little serifs on the bottom of the letters to help create kind of an imaginary line under the text. When you read Georgia, there's nothing about it that's difficult, and the typeface itself doesn't make you struggle through the material.

"No matter how cute, interesting, or unique a typeface you find, your body text needs to be something that is very easy to read and understand."

That's the goal of your typeface. No matter how cute, interesting, or unique a typeface you find, your body text needs to be something that is very easy to read and understand.

There are so many different typefaces available, and that's just for free.

There's even more that you can purchase that are designed uniquely by amazing and talented artists to help you express your written words in a way that is unique and different from everything else that's on the internet.

Unique is awesome, just not for your body text. The only job of your body text, and the typeface and font size that you choose is to make it easy to read.

That is the single filter that you need to put your decision through, and if the font and typeface don't make it as easy as possible, then you need to pick something else.

You can absolutely be unique in your headings, but the body text or paragraph text needs to be the easiest reading font that you can possibly use.

In most posts, the information that the user is coming for is going to be written in paragraph text or body text. That's where they're going to go.

If they have to suffer through some stylish cursive typeface, or an old script typeface, you might as well write the entire post in wingdings and have them use a cipher to figure it out.

Nobody's going to stick around, and you are going to annoy your readers to the point where they just leave.

The easiest way to pick out a good typeface for your body text is to pick a boring one. You read that right, just pick one of the normal, standard typefaces that's used for everything.

> *"The easiest way to pick out a good typeface for your body text is to pick a boring one."*

There's a reason it's used for everything, and that's because it's easy to read, it works, and it's what people expect.

There's nothing wrong with giving people what they expect, and when it comes to a body typeface, Arial, Georgia, Times New Roman, and Garamond are all good choices.

Use Creative Headers

If you must be creative, and you want to use a typeface that expresses a little bit of your individuality, then do it in your headings.

This is a place where you can use a typeface that is a little bit off the beaten path without having to worry about scaring everyone away.

After all, headings are very short, and they function as mini titles throughout your post for each section.

Since most titles are really quick, if you have an out of the ordinary typeface, it typically won't bother people enough to leave.

It may actually have an opposite effect of getting them to associate that particular typeface with your website. Once they associate your website with good answers, they may end up using that typeface as an indicator that they are at the right place.

While there is absolutely nothing wrong with just using a larger version of the same typeface that you use in your body text, if you do plan on getting a little creative, you can do so in your headings without distracting as much.

That's really the filter that you need to put this decision through. Are your headings distracting, or are they adding to the user experience? If they are adding to the user experience, or at bare minimum not taking anything away from it, then go ahead and use a different typeface that makes you happy.

"Are your headings distracting, or are they adding to the user experience?"

A word of caution though, make sure that the look you choose is still easy to read. Unless you have a very specific audience that is used a very specific look, you need to make sure that the typeface is easily readable. You also might need to look for an objective opinion to help you.

When it comes to typefaces, it's easy to fall in love with something, even though you know better. In a case like this, just bring the typeface to somebody else, and ask them to read a paragraph or two that's written in that particular typeface.

If they struggle, and you'll hear it right away, then it's not the best choice to use for your headings. In order to save yourself some time, write three different paragraphs with three different candidates for your heading typeface, and you'll likely be able to find at least one that's easy enough to read yet still creative enough to make you happy.

Bigger Spaces Between Lines

People are scared of large blocks of text that make it look like it's going to take a long time to get the information they came for. One of the ways to break this up is to use a larger space in between the lines of text in your paragraphs.

This is called leading, and it's a measurement of the amount of space between the bottom of one line of text and the bottom of the next line.

For a fun exercise, go into one of your blog posts, or create a draft with a bunch of random text that you copy and paste. Then, adjust the leading down to a very low number, and see with the text looks like. Even if it was very open, and easy to read in the beginning, it will now look like a solid block that is very intimidating.

Next, adjust the leading much higher than it was originally, and see the difference that the large amount of white space in between the lines of text makes. If this is your first time seeing so much space, don't let it be alarming. It doesn't look wrong, it just looks different to you.

A good ratio is to have a leading of around 1 1/2 times your font number. For example, if you are using a font of 18, use a leading of 24 to 26.

Basically you want to make it look like your lines are double spaced, or at least one and a half spaced. This keeps the text from bunching up, and it also helps you when you have to go back to the start of the next line.

If you've ever read a mass-market paperback book, they do the exact

"Dense writing is miserable to read."

opposite of this. They cram every single line of text as close together as possible in order to minimize the amount of paper that's required to produce the book.

That's one of the tricks for being able to sell a whole book for just a few dollars on a news stand.

These are miserable to read, and it's actually kind of difficult when you get to the end of a line of text to jump back to the beginning of the next one without losing your place.

Until you get used to this very dense spacing, you'll

end up going back and rereading the line that you already read, or accidentally skipping ahead too many lines and getting lost.

This breaks up the flow of your reading, and especially if you started to develop some momentum, and you were really getting into what you've read, it's just as bad as hearing a really loud noise and having it scare you out of the experience.

It can be shocking to run into a mistake like this as a reader and then have to get yourself back on track before you can immerse yourself back in the content.

It takes a way that magical feeling of really having the words permeate your mind, and it slaps you back into reality.

Instead of doing this to your readers, provide them with an ample amount of white space in between the lines of text so that way it's very easy to read from line to line.

This will also have a similar effect for encouraging scrolling just as using a larger font will. Since there is more space between the lines, less lines appear on the screen at the same time.

This means the user is going to have to scroll a lot more than they would before you increased the spacing.

"Scrolling is a positive signal to the brain that indicates to the reader that they are doing well."

As you've already heard several times, more scrolling is a positive signal to the brain that indicates to the reader that they are doing well.

Increase the amount of space between your lines, and you can help maintain a positive experience in your reader.

Use Excellent Grammar

The grammar that you use, and the way that the words come together are very important. If you use poor grammar, and your readers are attuned to what proper grammar looks like, it can be just as disruptive as losing their place as they read.

"Instead of enjoying the content, you are fixated briefly on the fact that the author doesn't know which witch is which."

Have you ever read a book and discovered a grammatical error? It stops you right in the middle of what you were doing, and focuses all of your thinking on that one error.

Instead of enjoying the content, or getting to the next part of the story, you are fixated briefly on the fact that the author doesn't know which witch is which. This is a huge distraction, because you're not writing a post about grammar, you're writing a post to try to help people solve their problem.

I'll confess that I'm not awesome when it comes to grammar, but when it comes to the obvious stuff, you need to go through and make the corrections necessary so that way your piece sounds as though it was written at an acceptable reading level for your audience.

This is where you have a little bit of leeway, and it's always best to cater to your audience when it comes to the level of grammar that you enforce.

For example, if you are dealing with academics, then your grammar needs to be on point.

These are the kinds of people that will notice when it's wrong, and it's not that you need to impress them or anything, you just need to make sure you don't distract them.

One way of distracting someone that knows there grammar really well is to write poorly. Even if your content and your ideas are outstanding, your poor grammar can bother someone enough that they stop reading, and at that point they get no benefit from all of your brilliance.

If you don't know something, look it up. There are so many resources online for basically anything you would ever want to know.

When it comes to grammar, all you need to do is type in what you're trying to figure out, and then apply the answer.

Use Smaller Words

No matter what type of audience you have, one of the ways to make it easier for them to read is to reduce the amount of thinking they have to do while they read. One of the easiest ways to do that is to use smaller words.

In most cases, using the smaller or the more common version of the word is the best choice. For example, instead of using the word utilize, just use the word use. It's the same thing, it's just a lot easier to read the word use instead of the word utilize.

This is also true of intentionally using language in an effort to make your text appear more educated, or more intelligent. In the majority of cases, anyone with a brain can see right through that. Not only will your sentences be more choppy, because the use of those words is not natural to you, it will also create a more difficult experience for your reader.

"Go through your writing and identify the words that slowed you down a little bit."

Depending on your education level, and the education level of your audience, you may have to make a conscious adjustment to the way that you write. That's okay though, because writing in a way that's easy to consume and making your audience happy is a surefire way to build their trust, and keep the readership.

If you are struggling with creating text that is easier to read for the average person, just go through your writing when you're done and identify the words that slowed you down a little bit.

Even though you know exactly what they mean, larger words in general will tend to slow you down. As you see these words, think about a way of replacing them that makes the sentence easier to read and understand.

Every time you do this, you make your text easier to consume. Even though the difference is a very small line by line, the overall difference is a feeling that helps your reader feel like they are at your level, and understanding what you are explaining.

As another example, have you ever watched a show on television or read a book that was just way over your head? Sometimes these are a little bit of fun, because you can make a game out of seeing how long you can last before they lose you.

As long as it's a game, and it's fun, you don't mind doing it. When you are struggling through a blog post to try to keep up with somebody who is obviously far more intelligent than you'll ever be, it's downright brutal.

Depending on the level of difficulty, it can cause you to leave long before you get the information you're looking for.

"Very intelligent people are still really good at reading small words. They are going to judge you based on your word choice, not the size of the words."

When in doubt, use the smaller and the more common version of the words that you choose, and you'll make the vast majority of people happy.

There is an analogy for this idea that has to do with fishing, and the size of the fishhook. When you use a large fishhook, you can only catch a large fish, because the small ones can't get it in their mouth.

However, when use a small fishhook you can catch any size of fish because they can all swallow it.

The same thing goes for your word choice. Very intelligent people are still really good at reading small words.

They are going to judge you based on your word choice, not the size of the words. This means you can use easier to read words in the right order and still satisfy the academics.

Also, people that may not know as many fancy words won't be excluded from enjoying and benefiting from your amazing ideas.

This is a double win, because the average person still gets to enjoy your writing, and the super educated person still gets to enjoy your writing.

Avoid Jargon When Possible

Something to pay close attention to when writing your blog posts is that you avoid the use of jargon when possible. Jargon is just the name for industry-specific terms that people outside of that realm wouldn't understand, or have any reason to know.

"Include a brief explanation of any jargon so that way people don't get lost."

This also includes any acronyms that are not completely obvious to the average reader. An example of a good acronym would be NASA, because basically everybody knows that means. An example of a poor choice in acronyms would be NPO which is a medical term for a patient who won't take anything by mouth.

Unless you are in the medical field, or you have a healthy interest in the medical field, you have no idea. Another bad example is NPC, which stands for a non-playable character in an online video game.

If you absolutely have to use jargon in your post, you need to include a brief explanation so that way people don't get lost, and stop reading out of confusion.

This is actually pretty easy, and you can just include the definition in parentheses after the piece of jargon or the acronym, and you only have to do this a couple times right in the beginning. After that, you can just use the word or phrase without having to constantly repeat what it means.

"You can completely eliminate the jargon or the acronym if you just replace it with something more common."

In many cases though, you can completely eliminate the jargon or the acronym if you just replace it with something more common. In the NPC example, all you would have to do is write non-playable character, or computer-controlled character instead.

This makes it very obvious to anyone who plays

video games that this is a character in the game that is controlled and operated by the computer, and that you cannot play as the gamer.

When it comes to high-end terminology, unless you are writing for a very specific and targeted audience that understands all of those words, it's best to either try to write them differently, or a bare minimum explain them after using the term.

One of the best examples of clearing up terms that don't immediately make sense is the TV show Star Trek.

Even if you're the type of person that does not watch science fiction shows, you can watch any random episode of Star Trek and completely understand what's going on.

The way the show was written, they are very good at subtly explaining what the different terms mean to the average person.

This means you don't need to have any type of background or understanding of science fiction in order to enjoy the show.

If you listen for it, you will hear them explain their terminology almost immediately after using it, and they do it in a way that is barely noticeable.

You can do the exact same thing in your posts, you just need to make sure that every piece of jargon or acronym is explained in a common sense way that the majority of people can understand.

Common Grammar is Allowed

The use of common grammar is allowed, and encouraged in your blog post as long as it makes sense, and it's understood by the majority of your readers.

A perfect example of this is the word ain't. For not

being a word, ain't sure gets used a lot. If you put this word in your text, people know what it means, even if it's technically not real.

There are lots of other good examples of common grammar, and it's a way to make your posts sound more conversational, and in the end more understandable.

"For not being a word, ain't sure gets used a lot."

The only thing to be careful for when using these types of words is that your readers understand them. If you have something that only works for a small section of people, and you're trying to appeal to a larger group, consider replacing that with the more commonly used version.

Use Lots of Contractions

Contractions are another excellent way of helping your reader gain speed as they consume your content, and it's really easy to do.

Instead of writing out every individual word, and never using contractions, which used to be the accepted method for any type of writing, you now just do the opposite.

In the end, it's far easier to read don't, we're, and you're than it is to read do not, we are, and you are. It's also easier to type, and if you dictate, your program will automatically put in the contractions as you say them.

There was a time long ago when the written word and the spoken word were very different. In some circles, this is still the case, but for the majority of writing, it's now acceptable to have it be more similar to speaking.

Contractions are a natural part of speech, and most people use contractions almost exclusively over the full phrases. This makes it really easy when you read, because you're reading something that you are used to hearing.

Familiarity is always good when it comes to reading, because when you're familiar with something, it doesn't scare you away, or make you nervous about continuing. You like what you're reading, it's comfortable, so you continue going.

When it comes time to edit your work, you don't need to go through your blog posts and combine every single word that

"Familiarity is always good when it comes to reading, because when you're familiar with something, it doesn't scare you away"

could be a contraction into a contraction.

Instead, just allow them to happen naturally, and resist the urge to separate everything out because you think that's how it's supposed to be.

Long gone are the days where the rules of writing are so rigid that you can't use contractions and be taken seriously. In reality, most of your readers won't even notice that you made a conscious decision to use them.

All they will notice is that the reading seems easy, and that they are not stopped or slowed down by the words on the page.

Use Accurate Spelling

There are so many things that can stop a person from reading, and you need to control as many of them as you possibly can. Some of them are well outside of your control, so it makes sense to focus on the things that you have closest to you. One of these is using accurate spelling.

Of all the things you have to do for your website, spelling things correctly is about as easy as it gets. The only thing it requires on your end is just reading and editing your work, and checking for those little red underlines that indicate misspellings.

Any content management system like WordPress will underline any obvious misspellings. This is the low hanging fruit when it comes to accurate spelling in your blog posts. Anyone with their eyes

"Your brain is a wonderful organ, and it's kind enough to change words into what they should be when you're editing."

open can see a word that's underlined in bright red, and make the decision to change it to the correct spelling.

The part where spelling gets a little bit more involved is when there are words that look the same, or very close, and yet they are not exactly correct.

An example would be the words though, through, and thought. When you're editing, especially if you're not going slow enough, all three of these words will become whichever of the three they need to be at the time to make your sentence make sense.

Your brain is a wonderful organ, and it's kind

enough to change words into what they should be when you're editing. Even though your brain has its heart in the right place, the results are still technically a lot of misspellings.

When you edit your work, you need to edit slow enough that you can catch all of the words that are technically spelled correctly on their own, but aren't spelled correctly in the context of the sentence in which they are used. This is where your big opportunity lies, not in the super obvious red underline words.

If you really want to catch all of your spelling mistakes, and you don't have someone else that can edit your work for you, there are a couple of different things that you can do to help yourself catch more mistakes.

First, change the typeface of your text to something different than you are used to, and increase the font size. Just seeing the material in a different look can help you find a lot more mistakes than seeing it the same way you wrote it. Once you correct everything, you can change that text back to the original typeface and font size.

Another thing you can do is just read your text out loud. When you read out loud, you see the words, say the words, and hear the words. This is

"When you read aloud as you edit, you have three chances to catch your mistakes."

three opportunities to catch your mistake, and it does make the self editing process a lot easier.

Finally, go through your work very slowly when you're looking for spelling mistakes. Especially spelling mistakes that are out of accidentally using a different but real word, your brain might just fool you into thinking that it's correct.

Don't let this happen to you, just combine a couple of these methods and you would be surprised at how easy it is to go through your work and catch all the things that you need to fix.

Besides, a spelling mistake is actually quite a disruption. Have you ever caught a spelling mistake in a book or blog pots? It stops you immediately, and you start focusing on that instead of the content.

"A spelling mistake is actually quite a disruption, and it can slow your reader significantly."

You start thinking...did the author really just make a spelling mistake in the section where he was telling you not to make spelling mistakes? Maybe it was intentional? Maybe it was placed there to illustrate the importance of spelling?

Either way, you have gotten off track, and are now thinking abut something completely different than the author has intended.

Bottom Line? Mistakes are distracting.

Instead of worrying about spelling mistakes, just change the font and typeface, read aloud, and read it slowly. Take a little extra time, and you'll be able to identify all of the mistakes that need to be corrected before you publish your post.

Write Conversationally

The difference between the written word and the spoken word have changed quite a bit over the years, and in the right direction. Now, writing conversationally is the encouraged method rather than writing properly.

By properly, I don't mean correctly, I mean proper as based on many of the volumes of stuffy text that teach you the right way to write English. These books are meant for scientific papers, academic essays, and other works where the format is more important it seems sometimes than the content. Thankfully, when it comes to writing for the web, it's more about having a conversation with your reader and giving them the best information than it is about using the proper in-text citation method.

Academic writing still holds a lot of these old standards for writing, but most bloggers are nowhere near this space. That's good, and it allows you to write conversationally.

Writing conversationally literally means writing as you speak. As an example, if you were to just have a conversation with one of your friends, and then record it, and transcribe it, you would have a written account that is conversational in tone.

That's because it came from a conversation.

If you've never written conversationally before, this can be a little bit of a challenge at first. However, all you need to do is work at it just like any other skill, and you will improve.

One of the easiest things you can do to make your

writing more conversational is to start dictating your blog posts instead of writing them by hand. There are several different amazing doors that open when you start dictating instead of writing, and one of those is writing more conversationally.

When you talk, or have a conversation, it's very conversational. I know that sounds funny, but all you need to do is talk to your computer and tell it what you want to say rather than write by hand. When you do this, you'll notice that your writing sounds a lot more like speaking, and it will be easier to read.

"All you need to do is talk to your computer and tell it what you want to say and your writing will sound far more conversational."

If you would rather not dictate, then pretend as you are writing that you are writing a letter to an old friend and telling them about your topic.

When you keep your friend in mind, you will write

differently because it's directly to them and not towards a nameless, faceless group of people. Your friend is your friend, so they are a lot easier to talk to in a way that is more natural.

As you work on making your writing more conversational, you'll notice that the words will also start coming to you a lot more easily. This is even more noticeable in dictation, because eventually you'll just start having conversations with your computer that turn into full-blown blog posts.

Your final test is just to read your post out loud as you edit, and make sure that it sounds like a letter to a friend. That's how you'll know your writing is on the right track.

Mixed Sentence Length

As you write, it's important to keep your reader entertained on a number of different levels. One of those ways is by making your writing come alive through varying your sentence length.

When you always write sentences of the same length, things can get boring. In order to combat that boredom, don't be afraid of writing sentences that are incredibly short, or incredibly long.

> *"When you always write sentences of the same length it gets boring."*

You don't want all of your sentences to be three words in length, and you don't want all of them to be 30 words in length either, but a healthy mix of everything is good for keeping your readers attention, and helping them focus on the text.

If you struggle with sentence length, just start using more commas. A comma is a great way of combining two short sentences into one longer sentence. You can even use several of them in a single sentence to create something even bigger.

Be careful that you don't create an overly long, run-on sentence, but even if you have to use a few commas in your writing before you end a sentence, it can help you create some variation.

Short sentences are good too. Every now and then, you need a short sentence to shake things up. Then, you can go back to your normal sentence structure. Just be sure to vary it every now and then so that way you can create some interest.

"Every now and then you need a short sentence to shake things up." If you work on your conversational writing, this part will actually come pretty naturally. In the course of the conversation, there are long sentences, medium sentences, and short sentences. It just kind of works out that way, so you don't really have to put a lot of work into it.

If this is completely new to you, just go back through your work and combine some of your shorter sentences, and chop down some of the longer ones.

Spend time reading your material out loud, and when it starts to sound droning, or repetitive, shake it up by altering the length of some of your sentences.

You'll like it better.

One Word Sentences

If you are really looking for a way to wake up your reader, try a couple one word sentences. Really.

They work, because they are different than what you expect, and they help you pay more attention to the content.

That's a good thing, because if your readers aren't paying attention, they could miss all of your awesomeness, and the answer that you are trying to give them.

One word sentences are pretty easy, in fact, they only take one word. Yep. One word sentences are super easy, so just try dropping one in every once in a while, just to keep things interesting.

Make sure you do this in a way that doesn't dramatically upset the flow of your material, but that subtly enhances your writing.

"Don't go nuts with one word sentences, otherwise you can agitate your readers."

If you go nuts with one word sentences, you can actually agitate your readers. For the same reason you don't want all of your sentences to be overly long, one word sentences eventually become distracting if they are in every paragraph.

The one word sentence should be seen almost like a trick that you pull out very rarely. It should be a surprise to your reader, but a good surprise that makes them more excited about continuing to read your content. Use them sparingly, and they will be super effective.

Use Transition Words

People like to be told how to do things. Whether they want to admit it or not, that's another story, but your readers love instructions. After all, they came to you for an answer, so an answer with instructions is even better.

This is where transition words are super effective, because they help knit your individual sentences together and create a larger body that is more cohesive and easier to see as one thing.

Examples of transition words are next, then, in addition, furthermore, first, and finally. There are so many more than just those of course, and it's a good idea to familiarize yourself with transition words because they just make your text easier to read.

In the end, that's the goal. Make your text is easy to read as possible, and people will continue reading. Use the right transition words, and you gently lead your reader from one sentence to the next without even realizing that they are being handed from one part of your content to another.

Imagine trying to write instructions for something without any transition words. It would be extremely boring, and it would be extremely difficult to follow. A recipe for example might say something like chop three onions, boil two carrots, stir until creamy.

However, the same recipe with transition words would sound more like this: First chop three onions, then boil two carrots, and stir until creamy.

Even just adding those simple little transition words between the instructions helps blend it all together into something that makes more sense, and is easier to follow.

When you add transition words into your own writing, you make it easier for people to understand the rhythm and the order of your words. You also help them see things like similarities, differences, likenesses, and contrasts.

The use of the right transition helps frame the mind of the reader for what's coming up, and when they expect to see what's coming up, and they are correct when it arrives, it creates a positive feeling.

"As a reader, when you confirm a suspicion, it makes you feel good."

For example, if I start a sentence with the word however, you know that what's coming is not the same as what you just read. You know that the however is a precursor for an opposite, or something that doesn't fit the previous sentence. When I deliver that opposite, and it confirms your suspicion, you feel good about it, and you keep reading.

Of course, all of this stuff happens in your head, and you really have no idea that it's happening because it happens so fast.

Your brain processes things at a rate that you can't even understand, but when you run into little ques like the ones that transition words provide, and then those suspicions are confirmed as you continue reading, it creates a sense of pleasure in the mind and a sense of agreement that helps build trust with the material.

Use more transition words in your writing, and you'll be happy with how much easier your material is to interact with for your readers.

Write in Active Voice

A great way to write blog post content is to use the active voice instead of the passive voice. The easiest way to remember this is to write live action instead of past action. This is where the subject of the sentence does something directly.

If you want to write about Henry eating some potatoes, write Henry ate the potatoes. The passive version of this would be the potatoes were eaten by Henry. Trust me, people are a lot more interested in Henry than they are in the potatoes. Make your post about Henry, and you'll be writing in the active voice.

"Trust me, people are a lot more interested in Henry than they are in the potatoes."

In the beginning, switching from passive voice to active voice can be a little difficult. It can also be a little bit difficult for you to notice when you are slipping into one and out of the other. This happens to writers all the time, so don't feel bad.

As you learn to write more conversationally, you'll also write more actively, because that is typically how you talk.

Spend a little bit of time reading your writing, and make sure that the subject does the action.

Also, as you write your sentences, write as direct of a sentence as you possibly can. This is another way that you can be sure you are writing actively.

Passive voice sentences sound like they are written in a roundabout way, with extra words that really aren't necessary.

When you eliminate unnecessary words from your writing, you create content that is easier to read, and can be read more quickly.

That's a huge bonus, because through one technique, using active voice, you satisfy two requirements.

You end up with a blog post that sounds like it's being written just for you, and you also end up with content that is easier to read. Double win.

Address the Reader Directly

One of the most frustrating things that you'll ever read in your entire life is when the reader is referred to as one instead of you.

One doesn't have to be a rocket scientist to feel how pretentious this style of writing is. It's much better to just address the reader directly, using the word you, and don't ever use the word one unless you referring to the number.

"One of the most frustrating things that you'll ever read in your entire life is when the reader is referred to as one instead of you."

I remember back in elementary school when I got in trouble for using the word you in an essay. Not only did I use it, I used the crap out of it.

As a result, I had to rewrite my paper and exchange the word you for the word one, which just never felt natural to me at all.

When I asked the teacher why, he told me that when I become an author, I can use you if I want, but now I need to use one. He never gave me an explanation of why it was important. He just said that I had to do it that way, so I did.

I don't even remember his name, but it would be fun to send him a stack of the nine books I've written and see if he remembers me from all the yous inside.

"If you want to form a bond with your readers, write as if you were talking to an old friend."

Thankfully, hard rules like not using the word you when addressing your reader are really not that important anymore. When you think about it, the word you makes the writing more personal, and since we are all people, we like when someone is personal.

If you want to form a bond with your readers, write as if you are writing to an old friend, just one person who you are helping solve one problem. Refer to that person as you, and it will help strengthen the bond between you and the people that read your content.

They will start to feel like you are talking directly to them in everything that you write and in everything that you create. It's a subtle way of building trust between each other, and it's an easier way of consuming the content as a reader.

Skip the Long Intro

Other than your two sentence intro, which is what I recommend as the very first couple lines in your blog post, you'll still more than likely do a small introduction right below that.

This is where you give a little bit more detailed of a preview of your content versus the two sentence intro that makes a promise for your readers if they continue reading.

The best piece of advice is to use three or four very short paragraphs to quickly and concisely explain what you are about to demonstrate in your post.

The purpose of an introduction is to tell your reader what you are about to tell them. This is the short version of the long story. Do everything you can to boil this down to three or four paragraphs that are only two or three sentences in length. Most people aren't going to read your introduction anyway, so don't frustrate the few that do by taking forever to tell them what you plan on telling them.

"Use the body content to explain and the introduction to introduce."

After all, you're about to give them the long-winded version coming up in the body of your post. There's no reason to have a gigantic introduction that almost gets to the point where it rivals the size of your content. Use the body content to explain, use the introduction to introduce.

Imagine an announcer coming on stage to introduce a fighter. Then, after saying the fighter's name he hops in the ring and starts fighting for him.

This is the same as when you do a very long introduction that reveals too much detail. The point of that announcer is to tell you the fighter's name, and a few stats about them.

After that, it's up to the fighter to actually do the fighting.

When you introduce your content, make a nice sweet introduction that previews the process, and what's coming up.

That's really all your reader needs, is just a little tip as to what's coming their way. They don't need anything more than that.

Keep it short, keep it interesting, and you'll keep your reader longer.

Add Captions to Images

When making your text easier to read, don't forget about making your images easier to read too. While you don't necessarily read images of course, you can enhance them by adding captions to further explain anything that might need some additional help.

It's a good idea to caption any image that isn't obviously explainable all by itself. You can also just make it habit to caption all of your images, and that can be a good practice too.

WordPress makes it very easy to add captions to your images. When you upload an image, in your media library there will be a space after you select the image where you can add a caption. All you need to do is type some information about that image in the space, and it will show up directly below the image on your blog post.

Another thing that you can do if you don't want to add captions directly beneath your images is to just explain them in the nearest paragraph. As the image comes up, and goes by, make sure that the text that is nearest to the image explains the content in the image.

This is the way that you can provide the same information that you would provide in a caption, but use it in a way that it lengthens your body text, and doesn't put any tiny writing below the picture.

It's a good practice not to go nuts when it comes to the amount of material that you have in your caption. It shouldn't be more than one or two very short sentences, and even two sentences is starting to get on the long side.

"It's good practice not to go nuts with the amount of content in your captions."

If you have to write that much, it's probably a good idea just to put that into the body of the post somewhere rather than try to load up the caption with everything you could possibly say about that picture.

You can also put links inside of captions, which is pretty cool if you want to include a call to action below your image.

This is great if you sell books or something else on your site, because you can show a picture of it, and then have a link below in the caption to buy it.

All you need to do is highlight the portion of text in the caption that you wish to turn into a link, and then click on the insert link tool in WordPress and paste the link just as if you were creating any other text link. The process itself is no different, the only part that changes is you select the text in the caption rather than some text from the body.

Use Bold Lettering Occasionally

When it comes to formatting the text of your post, it's important to do everything you can to make your post communicate well and be easy to read. One of these tools that you have is bold lettering.

Used on occasion, bold lettering is a great way of adding emphasis to certain words and phrases. It makes them easy to pick out of the group, and it gives the skimmer something to land on as they are flying through your text.

When used too often, the highlighting effect that bold text has diminishes. If you bold every third word in your post, you might as well not bold any of them

"Use bold sparingly. When everything is important, nothing is important."

because it's going to have the same effect. Using bold too often is a mistake, and in the end you're really not helping anyone by trying to make everything important.

Your readers are programmed to look at bold text as important text. When everything is important, nothing is important. Instead of using bold like crazy, try using a different technique like maybe creating a list of bullet points, or creating another section with its own bold header and normal text underneath.

Sometimes you have a lot of things to cover that are all fairly important, but you need to find a way to organize that information so it makes sense, and that doesn't make everything look important.

"Find a way to organize your information that makes sense, and you will need less bold text."

After all, some of those things carry more weight than others. That's where you can make sections, make lists, and then use bold type in a couple places.

If you've ever seen a website that uses bold lettering excessively, you'll know exactly what I mean. It is just miserable to try to read because each one of the bold words slows you down just a little until you realize that it's really not that important at all.

Then, you get going again, only to be startled by

another bold word or phrase, and you just repeat the process over and over again.

The efforts made by the writer to help you understand their post better become completely lost in the fact that it's just unnatural to read. It's not comfortable, so it's not a good user experience.

Use Italics Sparingly

You also have the ability to use italics in your blog post, though I recommend to use them sparingly. This means even less than bold text, and hardly at all if you can avoid it.

Italics are sometimes difficult to read, and on top of that, if you go nuts by trying to italicize every word that needs a little bit of extra emphasis, you end up creating a mess in your blog post that just looks bad when you see it on your device.

Your readers aren't stupid. They know where the emphasis should be as they are reading your post. If they don't, it's actually your fault, because you should be writing in a way that makes it very obvious where the emphasis needs to be.

There are exceptions to this rule of course, and in cases where you are trying to perhaps point out grammatical differences, or highlight differences between two sentences, then italics can have some utility.

They are also good for stylizing box quotes in text, which you can see me abusing heavily in this book.

Most people don't read books, they just buy them and wonder why their lives don't improve. I want you to get as much as possible from my writing, so I add quotes to hopefully hook you on a quote and lure you into reading the section.

I really want you to get value from my book, and adding interesting or intriguing quotes gives me more chances to actually teach you the material.

It sounds crazy that you likely won't read more than 10% of this book even though you paid for the whole thing. However, my job as an author is to get you to read as much as I can, and adding quotes does just that.

All of that being said, the use of italics for emphasis is definitely not needed. If you need emphasis, you just need to learn how to explain better. Do that, and you make your readers way happier than adding italics ever would.

"If you need emphasis, you just need to learn how to explain better."

Never Underline Text

Never underline text in your blog post. It's confusing, because links are underlined, and if you have something that really needs to be highlighted, perhaps you need to treat it in a different way or explain it better in order to give it the importance that it deserves.

On any modern blog post, words that are underlined are automatically interpreted by the reader as being links. When the reader moves their mouse over to that underlined text, and finds out that it doesn't go anywhere, it can be a significant letdown.

"Getting people to click on a link is not easy, so when you have people that want to do it, you absolutely have to give them the ability."

Links are an opportunity to join different pieces of content that have relevance to each other, and expand upon the ideas that are found in each post. When someone wants to click on a link, it needs to be there. Getting someone to click on a link is actually not that easy, so when you have people that want to do it, you absolutely have to give them the ability.

For this reason, it's important not to underline any

text in your post unless it's the underline that happens when you create a link in the text. This way, your site will function like all of the other sites on the internet, and the people who land there will be familiar with how it works, and not scared away because it's different.

Maintain a Proper Reading Level

There are a lot of different tools that you can use to assess the reading level of your material. Just do a quick Google search, and you'll find a number of different places where you can paste your post and get a score delivered to you for readability.

Why is readability important? You would be surprised at how little the average person reads, and as result how poorly they do it. It's important when you write your post that you write for the reading level of your audience, and even slightly lower.

It's important that you don't make yourself sound like an idiot, or sound like you're totally uneducated, but you do need to aim a little low in your writing.

If you feel like this is bad advice, don't. It actually comes from William Shakespeare. When he would write his plays, the language that he chose was that of the commoner, because he knew that the aristocrats would understand the common language, but the commoners wouldn't understand highly educated language. He wrote his plays for the groundlings, and everyone loved them.

"As verbally gifted as William Shakespeare was, he knew that writing in the language of the common person was the best way to appeal to everyone."

This was one of his secrets to creating plays that everyone could enjoy.

He wrote the language in a way that everyone could understand it, regardless of their education level. You can do the same thing with your blog posts, and write in a way that you don't scare away the readers who may not be as educated as you are.

Consider that the English language has about a quarter million words in the dictionary, and the average American has a working vocabulary of about 20,000 words.

This means that most people only know less than a 10th of the total amount of words available in the language.

It's also accepted that once you know about 10,000 English words, you can be considered fluent. That represents about 4% of the total words available.

If you stretch your vocabulary muscle, and create something that's difficult to read, the average person will just stop and find their answer somewhere else.

Write as if Speaking to a Friend

This is one of the best tricks that you can possibly use when writing your blog posts. If you want to write in a way that is very personal, and that creates a bond between you and your reader, write as if you are speaking to an old friend.

Write your post as if you were telling that old friend about it, or telling that friend how to do something.

The way that you speak to your friends, especially an old, dear, cherished friend, is very different than the way you would speak to a random person on the street. Even though your visitors are basically random people from the street, speaking to them like a friend starts to form a stronger bond right from the very first sentence.

Another thing you can do as you write is look at a picture of someone in the room. If you don't have a picture of someone, find a picture of someone that you love and respect, and put them on your desk, or near enough to you that you can see them easily.

As you write, look at them frequently, and write your post for them using the word you instead of using their name.

This is even easier if you dictate your posts, because you can basically stare at their picture the entire time and have a full-blown conversation with them while

"Dictate your post as you look at a picture of a friend near your computer."

your dictation program turns everything you say into words on your screen. It's super convenient to write this way, and it really allows you to speak directly to the person in that picture and write your post just for them.

If you've never written like this before, I urge you to give it a try. You would be surprised at how different your writing becomes when you change the nature or the reason for the writing.

Many times writing for a website or a blog can seem very impersonal, because you have no idea who your reader is.

You may meet some of them in the future, or have email correspondence with some of them, but it's very different. It's still people, but it's people that are constantly changing, so it's not really a person, but a collection of people that can be called your readers.

"Your blog is not one person, but a collection of people that can be called your readers."

Readers is a really abstract term for a lot of people, and you may have a hard time understanding. It's almost like looking at a car in terms of all of its parts. You can change out parts of a car one at a time, eventually replacing every single one of them, but in the end you still have the same car. That's kind of like your blog readers, they are always people, but they will nearly always be different people.

When you write for one person, staring right at a picture of a person that you love, the writing will be different, and you'll see it immediately.

Don't Repeat the Same Word Often

This is a problem that many new writers encounter, but it's really easy to solve. When you edit, pay attention to using the same word to close to another use of that word.

Instead of saying something like the car was so big that it was too big for the garage, substitute the word big and instead say that the car was so tall that it was too big for the garage.

It's not that either of those words were incorrect, you just don't want to use the same word over and over again.

When you vary the words that you use, and you

introduce synonyms that are still easy to say, read, and understand, you enrich your writing in a way that makes it more entertaining for your readers. In doing so, you keep them interested, and they will read more.

When you are dictating, it can be a little bit difficult to notice that you are using the same words too close together. When you go back to edit later on however, you'll notice that they are really easy to pick out.

"Diverse word choices make your writing more enriched and more entertaining to read."

When you see a sentence or a couple of sentences that use the same word in a way that seems too repetitive, just swap out one of those words with a synonym and you'll be all set.

Over time, this will become a natural part of your editing process, and you will diversify and enrich the quality of your written words every single time that you do it.

If you are struggling with vocabulary, it's a good idea to pick up a book or two and increase the number of words that you command. In the beginning it can be a little bit of a slow process, but if you commit to learning a few new words every week, you'll be ahead of the game very quickly.

Don't Begin With the Same Word Often

It's easy to begin sentences with the same word and not realize that you're doing it. Only when you go back and edit do you realize that you started two or three sentences in a row with the exact same word.

This only becomes a problem when it's noticeable, and just about any instance of three or more is going to be noticeable.

As you edit, pay attention to the beginnings of your sentences, and look for instances where you use the same word to start two sentences or more. If at all possible, and if it doesn't break up the conversational nature of your writing, choose a different word to begin one of those sentences. You can even split up a series of three by changing the start of the middle sentence.

Watch for Heavy Word Use

Finally, it's important as you edit to look for instances of excessively heavy word use. For example, you may use the word actually a lot. This is pretty common for new writers, and those who have to explain something to somebody else.

"Once a single word distracts your readers, you've lost them."

The word actually is a really good placeholder and it helps you demonstrate your knowledge. It's also really easy to use the heck out of it, and get to the point where it's almost comical. Once a single word distracts your reader, you've lost them. Now, instead of consuming your amazing work, they are more interested in seeing how many times you're actually going to write the word actually. It becomes almost a game, and they laugh every single time they see the word.

As this is happening, they are no longer absorbing or understanding the material that you're presenting.

You've lost them, and even though they're still reading, they're now doing it for entertainment of a different type.

You may get a little extra dwell time out of it, but they are going to go back to the search engine and pick a different result that doesn't distract them as much.

The only time that this should be of concern is when you easily notice a significantly higher word count for a particular word. If you are a little on the neurotic side, you can always paste your document into a word counter that will tell you how many instances of a specific word are found.

Don't pay any attention to the small linking words like a, and, or the. You are going to use these all the time, and it's not something that people notice as a repetitive words.

However, bigger words like important, understand, actually, and information will stick out like a sore thumb when you use them too much.

"Your big goal is that your words almost disappear, and it feels to the reader like you are telling them a story"

Again, if you don't notice it by reading it, and you can have a friend read the post and they don't notice it either, then it really doesn't matter what the actual count says.

What matters is that people are not distracted by your words. Your big goal is that your words almost disappear, and it feels to the reader like you are telling them a story. Repeating the same word over and over is a sure way to miss that big goal every single time.

Tips and Tricks for Writing and Typography

Here are a few tips and tricks for writing and typography that will help you:

- Write your content in a way that is easy to read, easy to see, and doesn't slow your reader down in any way.

- Use large fonts, easy-to-read typefaces, and wide open spaces in between the lines of text on the screen.

- Pay attention to your grammar and spelling, and use smaller words when possible.

- If you have to use jargon, clearly explain what it means right after using the word.

- Write conversationally, in active voice, using transitions, and writing like you are speaking to one person that you really care about.

- Maintain a proper reading level for your audience, and don't be afraid to aim a little low so that way everyone is included.

Chapter Three

Post Layout and Elements

This part of the book is all about the formatting elements of your post, and how you organize the words so they deliver the message effectively.

Again, it's about structuring your post and laying out the different elements in a way that makes it very easy for your reader to consume the content.

The goal is to make it as easy as possible, as friendly as possible, and completely erase any feeling that may be off putting in your layout.

There are a lot of different ways to do this, and they are actually pretty easy when it comes time to format your post. These are simple formatting methods that make your post easier to read, and encourage people to stay longer.

These include things like using shorter paragraphs, making lots of sections with their own headings, how you justify your paragraphs, and how you organize the text on the screen.

"There are lots of easy ways to format your words on the screen so they are easy to read and enjoy."

Each one of these is important, and they can help keep your reader longer.

Use Lots of Sub Headings

One of the easiest ways that you can break up your content into more manageable pieces is through the use of subheadings. Subheadings are ways of identifying certain sections and essentially creating mini titles for each one of those sections.

Headings carry a different amount of weight or importance when it comes to the creation of a document and how search engines handle their use. This means a heading one (H1) is considered more important than a heading two (H2), which is more important than a heading three (H3), and so on and so forth.

Through the intelligent use of headings, you can create lots of different sections throughout your blog post in order to transform a long and perceptibly miserable block of content into several smaller blocks.

Even though this doesn't do anything at all to

change the amount of words that are on the page, and in fact it actually adds more, the visual weight will be significantly less, and that will encourage people to read.

"Using headings significantly reduces the visual weight of the post, making it appear easier to read and navigate."

There are a lot of different strategies when it comes to using headings to break up your content, so if you are very interested in the search engine optimization the side of headings, then I recommend you look into that particular branch of blogging before you decide to move forward.

However, if you looking for an easy button, it's a good idea to have one heading one tag in your post, several heading twos, and several heading threes.

This will help you organize your information really well. The heading one is the most important section, then the heading twos are all equally important, and the heading threes are a little bit less important.

If this seems like a little too much to worry about, take a look at the next section coming up. This method of organizing your post is really just about creating many sections with their own tiny headline so that the skimmers can have an easier time finding what they're looking for.

You can assign everything a heading two if you like, and that will create a nice bold title right above the section for you. Just like that, you can solve your headings without letting it drive you nuts.

Create Short Sections

The big goal of post formatting is to create short sections that each have their own heading at the top. This makes it really easy to skim your content, and it also creates organized little pockets of data that show readers exactly were to go to learn about a specific aspect of your post.

Just like all little headings that you are reading in this book, the headings act as road signs to tell your readers what the coming section is all about. Each of these sections is organized, and it delivers the message that's seen in the heading.

"Headings act as road signs to tell your readers what the coming section is all about."

When you write, think of your post in terms of bullet points. That's about the easiest way to explain it, and it really does help especially when it comes time to write an outline.

If you think of your post is a series of bullet points, the first one would be the introduction. Then the next one would be your first main point, then your second main point is another. This is followed by your third, fourth, and as far down as you need to go to make all of your big points. Then, your last point is your conclusion.

Each one of these main points is a section. All you need to do is create a heading that says your main point, and then underneath that heading you take 3 to 5 short paragraphs and explain it.

Then, you go to the next main point, and treat it the exact same way. Write a heading that reveals the point, then again write 3 to 5 short paragraphs to explain it.

Continue repeating this process over and over until you get to the end of your post. When you look back, instead of seeing a gigantic column of text that goes from point to point to point without any clear separation between them, you'll see a beautiful string of segments that are each organized to present a certain section of the content.

This is a beauty to behold, especially if you've been typing a large column of text with no breaks. You can clearly look at this post format, and look back at your own and see the advantage to having sections and subheadings instead of a large column.

The real beauty of this type of writing is what happens for your readers.

Let's say you wrote an article on baking a cake, and there is a section on how to make your grand mothers frosting recipe. The person that's just looking for the frosting is going to skim through until they find that part of the post.

"Using headings makes it easier for the reader to find what they are looking for no matter where it's located inside the post."

Logically, for anyone who's ever made a cake, the frosting section should be at the end. However, since you are using headings and smaller sections, it will be super easy for your reader to find that particular part of the post, no matter where you decide to present it.

This goes back to one of the big ideas about blogging, and that's to make it as easy as possible for your reader to find the information they are looking for. You may not know it when you write a post about making a cake, but there will be people that come to your post for reasons that you did not anticipate.

They might have arrived just to see what type of pans you need to use to make a cake. Also, they may have landed on your page just to see the cake recipe. They may never even have an intention of making a cake, and they might just be there to demonstrate the process for someone else.

You really don't know why people show up on your website some of the time, so sections and organization make it very easy for people to find what they want, no matter how bizarre or off-the-wall it may sound to you.

"There will be people that arrive on your site for reasons that you cannot anticipate. Headings will help them find what they need."

There are a few little rules about sections that can

help you incorporate this into your post formatting process.

First, don't ever make a section that's longer than a couple hundred words. If you think about it, you can break up sections pretty easily, and even stuff that's closely related can still be broken up. The more you dissect your content into smaller chunks, the easier it will be for your readers to find with her looking for.

Next, don't make your sections so short that they look ridiculous. You should aim for about 3 to 5 paragraphs of 2 to 4 sentences each for every section. This is short enough that it's not overwhelming, but it's plenty of room to work if you have to explain the concept.

If it's not enough room, then you need to break that idea down into smaller parts and explain them in each one of their own sections. This may sound like a lot of work for you, but it will actually be quite a relief for your reader.

If you are explaining something complex, they probably arrived on your site because they have no idea how to do it themselves. When you break things down into smaller sections, it may seem simple for you but it might be just what your reader needed to finally understand the concept.

If you can give your post readers a win like that, they will begin to trust you, and in turn they will start consuming more of your content.

"Especially with something complex, your reader likely arrived on your site because they have no idea how to do it themselves."

Write Short Sentences

Short sentences are easier to read than long sentences. They are also less intimidating than long sentences, and in turn they can help your readers stick around longer.

I am super guilty when it comes to long sentences, which you probably already noticed. However, I am smart enough to know that shorter sentences do make a difference for your reader. I also make efforts to shorten some of them when I notice that they are getting far too long.

"Long sentences just aren't for everyone."

You should do the same, and even though you may have some longer sentences in there, it's good to split them up if they get out of hand.

There are some search engine optimization plug-ins for WordPress that will identify long sentences for you. If you are very concerned about long sentences, use a plug-in like this to identify and chop those sentences into smaller bits.

Going back to the attention span of the average person, and the reading and comprehension level of the average person, long sentences just aren't for everyone.

The fact that you are a writer gives me a little bit more leeway when it comes to sentence length, however for most genres shorter sentences are definitely the way to go.

Aim for the majority of your sentences to be around 15 words or less, with many of them being in the 5 to 10 word range. This way, you can have some that are longer, some that are shorter, and have a nice mix of sentence lengths that keep your posts interesting.More important than your individual sentences however is your paragraph length, and that's coming up next.

Write Short Paragraphs

More important than writing short sentences, and a little bit more impactful is writing short paragraphs.

Nothing looks more intimidating than a gigantic paragraph. I know it sounds silly, especially when you are writing for people that are looking to read, but a giant paragraph just turns people off.

"Most people will actually skip a large block of text just because they don't believe it's worth their time to read."

The problem isn't that you don't have great information in that giant paragraph.

The problem is that your readers don't know whether or not you have great information in that giant paragraph.

Due to that reason, most people will actually skip reading a big paragraph or large block of text just because they don't believe it's worth their time.

The average reader thinks that it's just not worth reading a large paragraph based on the chance that the information they are looking for won't be inside.

Instead of reading all of that content, they skip it, which is not the behavior you want to encourage.

In their minds, if they read along paragraph and don't get what they're looking for, they just wasted a bunch of their own time.

In reality, when you're surfing on your phone, you have a lot more time than you probably realize. This is part of the issue with time. It's subjective to the person experiencing it.

> *"In the mind of your reader, if they read along paragraph and don't get what they were looking for, they just wasted a bunch of their own time."*

Even so, breaking up your paragraphs into smaller sections makes it appear like it's an easier meal.

If you think about it, the amount of words and the amount sentences will be exactly the same in one giant paragraph as it would be in 10 smaller paragraphs.

As long as you don't add any material, and you don't take any material way, the amount of reading is still the same.

It's almost like going to a restaurant and asking that your large pizza be cut in five slices because you don't think you can eat ten slices. It still the same amount of pizza, no matter how you cut it up.

However, psychologically there's just something about a bunch of cute little paragraphs that makes them look less intimidating, and encourages people to keep on reading.

"There is just something about a bunch of cute little paragraphs that makes them seem less intimidating."

Don't worry about the psychology so much, just know that this method works really well, and if you go through your post and break it apart into smaller paragraphs, you will help your reader have an easier time consuming the good stuff.

A small note on how to break up your paragraphs, because this can be a little intimidating at first. If you've been writing for a long time, you've been programmed that a new paragraph is a new thought or a new idea.

You need to let go of that idea right now.

"You've been programmed that a new paragraph means a new thought. Let go of that idea right now."

A new paragraph just means a little bit more white space on your post. Don't worry about where to cut them off, or if you are extending the same thought into the next paragraph. People are just going to keep on reading.

At this point, you are more concerned about the format, and making the reading look very easy than you are about keeping certain ideas grouped together.

There are a lot of bloggers that write one or two sentences for every paragraph and that's it. They never consider the ideas in those sentences, it's just a hard rule. One or two sentences, and that's a paragraph. Their entire website will not have a single paragraph that has three sentences, no matter how long or how detailed their ideas become.

I recommend creating a new paragraph after about 2 to 4 sentences. You don't really need much more than that, and unless you have some really short sentences in there, I don't recommend going beyond four. You can sometimes, just keep it low.

Once you get used to writing like this, actually become second nature.

You'll open your paragraph with your first sentence, drop in one or two more, and then you're on to the next paragraph. You'll be able to do that over and over again, and it will be really easy to fill your subsections with text.

Left Align Text or Justify

There are a few different ways to align your text in WordPress, but there's really only two of them that you need to pay attention to.

Left align, and justify are the only two ways that you should align your text on your website.

No matter how much you like it, do not center the text or align it to the right. Your readers are used to reading text that is aligned on the left hand margin, or that justifies to both margins equally.

"Left align and justify are the only two ways you should align text on your website."

Anything other than that is going to be confusing, it's going to slow them down, and they are going to leave faster than they should.

The easiest way to do this is just to make the decision early on as to which type of alignment is going to be your particular style. It really doesn't matter which one of the two you choose, it just matters that you pick one and you stick with it.

It's more important to be consistent with one type of alignment than it is to pick left or pick justified. In reality, they both look good. They also give the reader something they are familiar with, and something that's easy for them to read.

Allow Lots of White Space

Resist the urge that you may have to fill every last available square inch of your blog with something.

This is a recipe for failure, because it creates too much, with too many distractions. One of the best things that you could possibly do is allow lots of white space to naturally occur on your post.

White space is simply the term for an area of your

post or your site that doesn't have any content. The background of your website is typically white, so that's where the term comes from.

Technically, it actually comes from the white background that books are printed on, but it's been carried over to the website realm as well.

> *"Just because there isn't anything there, doesn't mean there is anything wrong."*

Just because there isn't anything there doesn't mean there's anything wrong. Read that again. Just because there isn't anything there, and you're seeing some white space, doesn't mean you need to rush out and fill that section of your page.

In fact, white space is actually encouraging to your readers, and it helps make your page look less intimidating. Yes, you can have a page with so many things on it that it actually intimidates your readers.

While they are not actually afraid of your webpage,

they are afraid that is going to be too difficult to extract the one little nugget of information they came to find.

That's where you lose your readers.

If you have too many things going on, and your website doesn't look simple enough, most people just won't feel like they can find the one little scrap of information that they want without having to dig through a huge mess.

When it really comes down to it, most of these readers are going to back out of your site and go pick another result that appears to be less of a challenge.

In order to combat this, resist the urge to fill every nook and cranny on your webpages and your blog posts. Allow some space to appear naturally, and don't worry if your page actually looks a little bit bare on desktop.

Most of your users are going to be on mobile anyway, so a lot of that white space is actually going to disappear.

One easy way of increasing the white space is to increase the space between the lines of text, which was discussed in the previous chapter.

Increasing the amount of spacing between your lines allows more of the white background to come through, and it appears that there is less that you have to read. This is a positive signal most people, and it can keep them on your site longer.

Another thing that you can do is center align your images so that way they are buffered on both sides with big blocks of white.

You can also format your images with a white border around them, and when you place this on a white background, it will have the effect of pushing the text farther away from the image.

This can be good if you use left or right justified images with a text wrap.

"Don't feel like you need to fill every blank space on your site to be successful."

You can also do things like adding larger blocks of text or quotes that will naturally create padding above and below itself and increase the white space.

Allow white space to happen naturally, and don't feel like you need to fill every square inch of your site to be successful.

Use Lists and Bullets

Another formatting trick that is super helpful for helping your readers find the information they are looking for is lists and bullets.

These make organizing your information very simple, and they are really effective when you have to deliver a series of steps.

Instead of writing out paragraphs, try adding some bulleted lists or some numbered lists instead. It's simply a matter of highlighting the text, and clicking on the bullets or the numbering.

Suddenly, this string of sentences becomes an organized list. It immediately draws your attention, and appears to have more authority.

A great way to incorporate lists and bullets into your post is to do a tips and tricks section. People love tips, tricks, and hacks.

Just about any keyword that you write about will also have that keyword with either tips, tricks, hacks, or all three as an alternative keyword. If you provide this information in a section of your post, you'll give the search engines yet another reason to return your website in the results.

All you have to do is think of your own experience with what you are teaching, and help them avoid some of the mistakes and pitfalls that are associated with it. This is usually the nature of tips and tricks. It's about avoiding mistakes that beginners typically make.

If you have to give someone a series of steps for accomplishing something, such as a how-to article, you can use the numbered list to give them a quick version of what they need to do.

"A list is a great way to show a condensed version of a series of steps, and it's visually appealing too."

Break the steps down your mind, and write them out in a list format. This makes it really easy for your reader to see exactly what they're going to need to do, and it also gives them the order in which they need to do it.

Bulleted lists are also a good way to break up the monotony of the blog post.

If you have a lot of sections, it can get a little boring seeing heading / content, heading / content, over and over again. One way you can break that up is with a bulleted list or a numbered list.

Break Up Large Blocks of Text

It's important to go through your post when you're done, and look for any sections of text that got away from you. Odds are, in the beginning, you'll find several opportunities to improve the way that your post looks.

One of these big opportunities will come after you insert your images. All of a sudden, once the text wraps around an image, the words will look a lot taller and a lot more intimidating than they once did.

This is your opportunity to break up that paragraph into a couple smaller paragraphs.

The most important place that you can look for intimidating sections of text is on mobile. Since most of your readers are going to consume the content on their smart phone, it's important that you look at the way your site renders the phone.

Paragraphs that seem short and sweet on desktop also have the advantage of at least a 15 inch monitor to spread out your message. On a phone, you only have a couple inches to work with, so even small paragraphs can get kind of big.

"Even small paragraphs can get kind of big on mobile."

View your post on mobile, and make the adjustments necessary to ensure that your text doesn't scare anyone, and that you are doing everything possible to ensure the promise of a good reading experience for everyone who visits.

I promise, it's worth the extra effort. Most people just stop reading altogether when they come to a large paragraph without any breaks.

There's just no attention span anymore, and in order to keep your readers, you have to modify the way that you present your material to counteract that.That's right. Don't lament the death of reading. It's your job to get them to read even though the don't want to.

Add Pull / Block Quotes

Pull or block quotes are an easy way to break up your text without a lot of effort. This also gives you the ability to highlight different sections of material.

The text will appear larger, and in a highlighted manner, which can encourage your readers who skim to at least read these particular sections.

"Quotes are a great way to break up your text without a lot of effort."

WordPress allows you to do quotes right out of the box, but there are also other plug-ins that you can install that will help. If you use the standard WordPress option, all you need to do is highlight the text and then press the quote button on the toolbar.

WordPress will do the rest, and you'll have a fantastic quote right in the middle of your post.

Just like anything awesome, you can overdo it.

Quotes should be like a garnish, or a dash of the spice that makes your dish perfect. You definitely don't want to use this too often, otherwise it can look like the majority of your site is made up of quotes.

One of the easiest things to do with quotes is just use them to highlight pieces of information that you know are super important. Just select some text that mentions that bit of information you want to feature, and then turn it into a quote.

If you are just using quotes to break up large paragraphs, and inject some more interest into your post, then all you need to do is pick a relevant sentence, or a main idea sentence and turn it into a quote.

Spend a little bit of time picking the right ones that will make sense, but then just turn it into a quote and it will do its job.

Add Images

Poeple are visual. They like images, and they like to see images on blog posts. This is one of the key formatting items that you absolutely have to pay attention to.

"People like to see images on blog posts."

Yes, there are rare blogs that succeed without images. However, there are usually other reasons that support their success and it's definitely not because they don't have images.

Images serve a purpose to help communicate what's going on in your post in a different way. If done well, sometimes a post can stand alone just on the images, without reading a single word.

In the case of the tutorial for example, if your pictures are taken well enough, and they demonstrate the steps properly, then you might not have to write very much in the post at all in order for the reader to receive the message.

This is awesome, because it means that you are communicating really well on a couple different levels. When your communication is this good, people will spend a lot of time on your site, and that's a good thing for you and for them.

Not only do your images need to represent your topic, and your post, they also need to be made in a way that they are easy to understand.

Also, the files need to be modified so that way they are light and quick loading. There are a lot of different options for editing photos, and they range from completely free to very expensive.

As a beginning blogger, I recommend that you start with some of the free options, and then only work into paid choices if you absolutely must.

There's enough free stuff out there to edit, crop, and re-size your images that you can probably go your entire blogging career without paying a dime for that service.

"As a beginner, I definitely recommend starting out with the free options for editing your photos."

Once your images are made well, and they are small file sizes for quick loading, upload them to WordPress and then insert them where they make the most sense in your post.

It's okay to go a few paragraphs or even a couple sections without an image. You just don't want to go too far without giving person a little break from reading and showing them something to see instead.

Use as many pictures as you need to communicate your message, and at a bare minimum you should have at least one image for every one of your blog posts.

When it comes to making your own images, you definitely want to avoid the stock photo sites is much as possible and instead just use your camera phone to take relevant pictures yourself.

"Use as many pictures as you need to communicate your message."

No matter what type of blogging you do, there is a way to take relevant pictures with your phone.

They may not be of the exact content that you are writing about, but they can be related enough that they make sense.

In the end, generic pictures that are loosely related are sometimes all you need because you can team them up with some lettering as an overlay, and you'll have a really nice graphic that doesn't look out of place on your post.

Use images often, and use them in a way that breaks up the monotony of reading. Your readers will be happy, and they will stay on your post longer.

Black Text on White Background

The absolute best tip that you can take away when it comes to post formatting comes from the millions and millions of books that are already in print.

People are used to reading black text on a white background. On your blog, you need to have black text on a white background in order to remain congruent with what people are used to.

This is actually really easy because most themes are set up like this right from the start. There are a few rare exceptions that use a different color of text and a different background, but the majority will be black text on a white background.

This is good for a lot of reasons, and the first is that people are used to this format. Next, it's also easier on the eyes especially when compared to white text on a black background.

When it comes to colorful text, while this may seem whimsical and fun at first, it can actually be very difficult to read.

> *"Black text on a white background is the best way to write your blog posts to make them easy to read."*

If there's not enough contrast between the text color and the background, it causes a strain on the eyes, and a user that feels strained or fatigued is going to leave. You can also run into a situation where there's too much contrast, or the colors clash, and that can also cause readers to run away.

The easiest way to make sure that your readers get what they expect, and that you provide the type of experience that they like is to keep it simple, and keep your text black and your background white.

If you do want to experiment with different colors of text, you can always have a little fun with your logo, or you can have a little fun with the text overlays that you place on your images.

You still need to be careful that these are easy to read, but they are a small area of your site when compared to the body, which is the majority of the space.

The backgrounds don't have to be dead black and dead white, as long as they are a shade of each that is close to pure.

For example, you are reading black text on cream paper right now, and it's not difficult. If the text were white and the paper were gray, you wouldn't have made it this far into the book.

Narrow Your Content Column

Another fun trick to build momentum for your readers and help them scroll faster is to narrow your main content column. This works more on desktop than on mobile, because on mobile it will already be narrowed significantly.

If you think of your main column as a container, you can adjust the width of the container and the contents will just stretch out. If you make a container wider, your sentences will be longer before jumping down to the next line.

"The narrow column is better than the wide column because more length populates for the same amount of words."

If you're container is narrower, then less words will populate in the sentence before the next line appears below.

The narrow column is better than the wide column because you'll get people to scroll more, and dive deeper into your site.

In reality, they're not actually getting any farther

than they would with a wider container, it just feels that way.

However, that's a really good feeling, and it keeps your readers excited about continuing their journey. Psychologically, they feel like they are dominating your website, and a slightly narrower column can do that.

Be careful when adjusting your container witdth in your theme, because if you make it too narrow, it can look ridiculous.

A good idea is to reduce the size by about 20%, which is enough to make a difference, but not enough to stand out. You can push it to 30%, but at this point is going to start to be noticeable.

It doesn't really matter that your readers notice it's different, but it does matter if they think that there is something wrong. This is where keeping your container somewhere near the normal size for a standard website is a good thing.

Using some of your existing material for a reference, experiment with different container sizes and see how it affects your layout on desktop. Play around until you find something that you like, and a narrower container can help you keep your reader moving.

Tips and Tricks for Post Layout and Elements

Here are some tips and tricks for your post layout and the different elements that appear on the page:

- Use lots of subheadings to create small sections within your post. This is much better than a large block of text, and less intimidating.

- Write short sentences with short paragraphs.

- Don't be afraid to break up paragraphs right in

the middle if needed.

- Use different techniques to create white space, and don't be worried if there is a lot of white space in your post.

- Bulleted lists, numbered lists, and quotes can help you add interesting elements to your content and break up any long sections.

- Add enough images that you help your reader by showing a visual representation of what you are talking about with your text.

- Take your cue from all the books in the world, and use black text on a white background for the body of your blog post.

Chapter Four

Design and Navigation

When it comes to the design and the navigation of your site, you can spend countless hours modifying little things here and there.

If it's not one thing, it's another, and you there are so many different elements that you can spend a lot of time working on design.

It's a black hole that will suck all the content creating time right out of you if you let it.

"Design is a black hole that will suck all the content creation time out of you if you allow it."

However, there are some basics that you need to get right in order to be successful. These basic design and navigation elements are expected on all sites, and they are expected by your readers that visit your site too.

First of all, I recommend that you spend far more time on the navigation and the usability of your site than you do on the design.

In the beginning, it's better to have a good user experience with an average design than it is to have a killer design with an awful menu.

Start your focus there, and once you have a design and navigation that are simple, and easy to understand, you can be done with these two things for quite some time.

After all, in the beginning it's more important to focus on getting traffic than it is to focus on your site design.

Keep Your Design Simple

The very first thing you should do when it comes to site design is decide right away that you want to keep things simple, and good-looking.

"It's much better to execute a simple design really well than an elaborate design poorly."

It is much better to execute a simple design really well then it is to barely make it through a complex design, or execute it poorly.

A simple design that's done really well will impress anyone who sees your website. On the other hand, if your design is more elaborate, but you don't deliver the basic features like usability, and easy navigation, then it will provide a poor experience for your readers.

That being said, take a look at the different options you have for themes, and pick a simple look that makes the design process very easy.

There are many clean looking themes, and one of the best is GeneratePress.

This is the theme that I use for all of my sites, and it's simple enough that you can get it to work right out of the box. It's also featured enough that you can make it do essentially anything you want in the future.

There is a free version, and then a paid plug-in which gives you all of the advanced features and allows you to manipulate more of your site. If you're first getting started, the free version will be fine for a while.

Beyond the simple theme, start thinking in terms of

the simple site that delivers what people are interested really in. People that visit your site are really interested in the information, and not as much in the way that it's presented.

"Google doesn't care about your site design as much as they care about the user getting the right answer."

For example, a website with a killer design and amazing navigation that doesn't have good information will eventually fall very far down the search rankings.

In contrast, I'm sure you've seen websites on page 1 of Google that just look hideous. Google doesn't care about your site design as much as they care that you are giving the information that is the most relevant to whatever search term user types in.

For this reason, remember that your design is something that will be appreciated, but only after the user gets the information they came for.

That being said, spend a little bit of time on site design, and just focus on creating something that is simple, and easy to maintain.

Keep Your Background Simple

The days of elaborate website backgrounds are pretty much gone. With such an emphasis now on loading times and site speed, any extraneous element that can be removed from your site probably should be removed.

The more things that have to load on your site before it can render for the user, the longer it's going to take. A background is no exception, and even a very light background with a small file size is still another file that has to load.

However, if you must have a background, keep it very simple, and keep the file size very small. Also, if you can restrict it to the far edges of your page on the left and right, and keep the section underneath your text white, then that's what I recommend.

Not all themes have containers, so your background might actually show underneath your text. That's definitely not what you want, unless the area directly beneath the text is white.

> *"Find a background image that tiles without being able to see that it is tiled."*

Also, when it comes to backgrounds, they tile to fill the area. This means there will be a line between the bottom of the first tile and the top of the next as you scroll the site. This can be pretty distracting.

If you are going to do a background image, find one where the bottom of the picture and the top of the picture blend together without a seam.

This will make it look like it's one continuous background without any gaps, even though it's actually being tiled by the computer.

Again, your primary goal when it comes to everything on your website is to make it easy for your reader to get the information they're looking for, and not distract them or annoy them in any way.

I'll tell you from first-hand experience, the gap in the tiling on a tacky looking background is really annoying, and it's a distraction that you just don't need on your site.

When in doubt, just leave the background white, or whatever color comes standard with your theme, which may be a very light shade of gray. Either way, it won't be a distraction, and it's one less thing to worry about loading with the rest of your site.

Wild Designs Are Hard to Read

Have you ever been to website that has a really over-the-top design? The colors are bizarre. The text looks weird, and the layout just doesn't match anything that you ever seen before. The unfortunate thing about these kinds of websites is that their owners tend to think they are masterpieces.

"The unfortunate thing about bizarre looking websites is that their owners think they are masterpieces."

This doesn't make them bad people, it just means they don't understand the fundamentals of web design and navigation.

Rule number one is to make it very easy for your reader. Anything that distracts from rule number one needs to go away.

If you do a Google search for crazy website design, or wild website design, you can find some examples of sites that are so elaborately styled that they lose all of their functionality.

These are not positive examples of course, so definitely remember that when you land on these sites.

However, even though these are extreme examples, you can veer that way on a smaller scale depending on the decisions you make for your site.

Instead of going that route, do everything you can to steer the boat closer to classic and simple at every chance you get.

This way, you'll never have to worry about someone leaving your site just because they had a difficult time getting around, or understanding what was going on.

Choose a Classic Color Scheme

There are a lot of different options for choosing a color scheme for your website. If you are interested in marketing or branding, then you definitely want to spend a little time looking into the psychology of color, and how it relates to your brand and ultimately your customers.

However, if you're looking for the easy button, just do a Google search for complementary design schemes, or complementary color schemes, and you'll find lots of different examples to work with.

All you need to do is pick out one of these sets of colors and implement them on your website.

"All you need to do is pick three colors and know that they go together really well."

You definitely don't need to use all of the colors that they recommend, because most graphic design sites are going to recommend about five different colors. All you need to do is pick maybe three at the most, and know that those three go together really well.

These can be the three core colors of your design, and you can work them into different areas of your site really easily. One of the easiest places to do this is on backgrounds for your images, or backgrounds for quotes.

You can also use these colors in your header and footer, which is a good place to experiment and showcase your brand and your colors.

Just as the site design should be simple and elegant, most color schemes that go together really well also satisfy the same requirement.

"Avoid colors that clash heavily or that cause a strain on the eyes when viewed on a computer."

Avoid colors that clash heavily, or that causes strain on the eyes. Some colors look great as swatches, but they look terrible on the computer.

Make sure wherever you find your colors, you first ensure that they look good on the computer as well.

You can even narrow your search to the most common colors used on a computer screen, that way you know that no matter who is viewing your content, they are viewing your colors just as you wish them to be seen.

The sooner you pick a set of colors for your website the better.

Especially if you use color quite a bit, it can be a lot of effort a few years down the road to completely re-brand and change your color scheme.

Instead of going through all that, take a little bit of time and think about the colors that most represent you and your brand.

Find a site that will generate pleasing colors to go with your main choice, and you have several good options to choose from.

Spend Minimal Time on Design

As a beginning blogger, and a busy blogger, you should spend very minimal time on site design. Once your site looks nice, and the navigation is good, all of your attention needs to be diverted to generating traffic.

No matter how beautiful your website is, nobody is ever going to see it if you don't have traffic.

The cause of, and the solution to nearly every problem that you have on your website is traffic.

If you're not getting a lot of clicks on your calls to action, you need more traffic. If you're not getting a lot of ad

"The cause of and the solution to nearly every problem on your website is traffic."

impressions because you don't have a lot of people landing on the site, you need more traffic.

Traffic is the problem, but traffic is also the solution.

Don't spend a lot of time on site design as a beginner. It's easy to dive into this elements of your website because it's just not as difficult as creating new content. The design side lures you in, and you feel like you are working.

This is a trap, because you feel like you're doing something important when you're really just doing something.

"Design is a trap, because you feel like you are doing something important when you are really just doing something."

You can literally waste your entire life messing around with site design, adding new elements, taking out old elements, and getting everything arranged just perfectly.

I'll tell you now, this is a complete and total waste of time.

There are one page websites online that get millions of viewers every single day, and their design is absolutely putrid.

The design definitely doesn't mean very much anymore, and as a beginner the only thing you should really care about is traffic.

Black and White Always Works

If you are absolutely stuck on a design for your site, or you are completely stumped on color, just go with black and white.

The nice thing about black-and-white is that they go with everything, and you'll always have black-and-white elements on your website, no matter which colors you eventually go with.

This means you can be free to go as far as you want with black and white, but when the day comes that you add color, you won't have anything to worry about, because it will still all match.

Starting out with black and white also gives you the opportunity to get started a lot faster, and with a lot less headaches. The faster you can get past creating a simple site, with a clean look, the faster you can get into generating content that brings in readers.

Once you have lots of happy readers, you'll be more

likely to be in a position where you can pay someone else to create a beautiful looking website that you wouldn't even be qualified to create anyway.

Even though you didn't do it yourself, you paid for it, so in a roundabout way you still did it.

"Even though you didn't do it yourself, you paid for it. So, in a roundabout way you did do it yourself."

There are also a lot of examples of very successful websites that have a simple, black and white color scheme. Going back to the page speed example, the less your server has to think to load your website the better.

Websites that are heavily text based, and that don't have any colored elements to load populate on the screen faster.

The speed at which you website loads as a direct impact on the behavior of your readers. It also sends signals to Google that your site is optimized with the user in mind. These are both good signals, and they come from keeping things simple.

One of the things you can keep simple right away is your color scheme. Start out with black and white, and you can always add more colors down the road.

You won't be locked into anything, and you won't have to worry about spending hundreds of hours in the future changing everything that you've built up to that point.

Mirror Existing Sites for Design

There are so many different websites on the internet, and if you are looking for some design inspiration, then you only need to browse for a little while to see plenty of it.

This is not stealing, as long as you don't directly copy some other person's exact layout. All you really need to do is look through several different websites and write down a list of the things that you like, so that way you can start incorporating them into your site.

"Even if you are in an interesting genre, your site will still likely have a similar look to others in your space."

After little while, you'll have a pretty comprehensive list that will keep you busy making your site beautiful.

I recommend that you look at other sites that are in your niche and start finding your inspiration there. This way, at least your site will be consistent with the other sites that are out there in the same space.

Most of the time, websites are pretty similar, and even if you are in an interesting genre, your site will still probably look similar to many others.

That's completely okay, because people like things that look familiar, so if your site design is too outlandish, it could scare people away.

Identify the top 10 sites in your niche, and one by one, start looking at how they are organized. Take a look at the different pages, check out the posts, and the blog roll. Look in their archives, and see how their menu is structured.

"On a good site, everything is where it is for a reason."

Spend a little time on the homepage digging around and seeing how it's laid out and organized.

What are the main things they are hoping you do when you are on their homepage? Is there an obvious place they hope you'll go? Look for their newsletter sign-ups, and their calls to action. Spend time getting to know where they put things, because everything is where it is for a reason.

Think about that last part again. On a well-established site, everything is where it is for a reason. It's no accident that things are placed where they are, and odds are there has been some research that's gone into that particular placement.

You can use this information to your advantage, because you can get a lot of the benefit without actually having to suffer through the research.

For example, you may notice on several of the top sites that a sign-up for the email list is at the very top of the sidebar. This is intentional, and the owner of that website believes this to be a high converting area for getting people to sign up.

You may also notice things like exit intent pop-ups that cover the screen right before you try to hit the back button. Where do these direct you? Are they giving something away? Selling? These are the questions that can help you find inspiration for designing your own website.

After you go through around 10 websites, and you write out a large number of things that you like, narrow down the list to the things that are the most important and start implementing those on your site. Make sure you still spend more time on traffic than you do on site design. However, when you do work on design, focusing like this on the best areas can give you the biggest return for your time.

Pages for Static Content

Blogs are organized into two main types of content, pages, and posts. These essentially create the same thing, it's just a slight difference in the way that they are handled by WordPress.

Pages are best for static content, or something that you want to add to the website but you don't necessarily want to show up in your feed.

"Pages are best for static content like Legal or About pages."

Your blog page will show all of your newest posts, so if you're publishing something like a disclaimer, or an About Me page, you want to use the page instead of the post, that we you can add it to the site without showing up in your timeline.

"WordPress lets you choose how visible your pages become."

When you're inside of WordPress, you'll see options for pages and posts on the left-hand side. This is where you can choose which element you create.

Again, it's going to create the exact same thing, a single web page, but the way that WordPress handles pages is that it basically allows you to choose how visible they become.

When you first start your blog, you're going to have to create several pages right from the start. These are the pages that are the most often associated with a website, and they include a homepage, about me page contact page, and more.

You may have pages that have legal disclaimers, a

newsletter sign up, and a place to see pictures of your upcoming events.

All of these are perfect candidates for pages, because it's a piece of content that doesn't need to be posted to your blog page, but needs to live somewhere else, like perhaps inside of the main menu.

When you post your recurring content, which is the stuff that your blog will mostly be made out of, this is when it's time to use the post feature.

Posts for New Content

When you create a post in WordPress, it lands right on the top of your blog page. This is a long single page that has your newest posts at the top, and gets older as you scroll down.

You can set it up a number of different ways, and you can even have it create additional pages instead of having one massive page, but it's basically the same thing. It's a running timeline of your content.

Let's say your blog is about dog walking. Anytime you write something new that deals with dog walking, or some aspect of dog walking, you want that to be in a post. This way, as users scroll through your blog archives, they can see that post, along with any other post on the subject all in one place.

Essentially, anything that you want to end up in your feed, you just go ahead and create a post, and it will be there.

You can separate your posts by categories, and break them up into their own little sections. However, when it comes to your blog, everything is just going to show up in chronological order with the newest stuff at the top.

This is the way the blog works. It's also the differentiating factor between a blog and a static website. Most websites have individual pages that don't create anything similar to a blog page where all your newest content shows up automatically.

With a blog however, it is expected to see content in this type of arrangement, and people that are familiar with blogs know how to scroll through to find the content they're interested in seeing.

There are many different ways to style your blog page, which will be the collection of your posts. I recommend that you make this page fairly

"Make your main blog page lighter by not showing the full post and by loading 3-6 posts before requiring a click to the next page."

light so that we loads quickly, and you can do that by only showing partial posts instead of full content, and limiting the page to about three to six posts in total.

If you try to load the full post, especially when you write long form content, your user can get tired of scrolling before they even get a couple posts into your blog.

In order to combat that, all you need to display is a summary and a picture, which will show right below the post title, and that should give any reader plenty of information to decide whether to click or not.

Also, reducing the number of posts that load on each page before you have to click to go to the next page at the bottom is a good idea too.

This means your server will only have to load a handful of posts before the page is complete. At that point, when the user clicks to advance to the next page, it loads the same number, and the page speed stays quick.

You can also experiment with laying out your pictures in more of a masonry grid style, which has been made popular by sites like Pinterest.

This is where your main images tile themselves near each other, and the image itself is what tells your readers what the blog post is about.

This works great when you use graphics with a picture and text over the top. This way, all you need to do is include the title, and your readers will know right away whether that article is interesting to them or not.

Have a Simple Main Menu

When it comes to the navigation on your website, the absolute best thing you can do is keep it very simple.

There is a huge temptation in the beginning to add every single page you create to

"When you give people too many choices, they tend to make no choice."

your main menu. This is a mistake, because in general when you give people too many choices, they tend to make no choice.

That's the worst thing that could happen, because in

the end, you want people to keep clicking on your site as much as possible, because it means they are exploring around and getting a benefit from it.

"Keep your menu small by reducing the number of categories that you write about." The first thing that you need to do in order to keep your menu small is to keep the number of post categories that you have small.

In most genres, a website only address a small handful of individual things. These are categories within the category, and they are a way to break up and arrange the information in a more digestible manner.

If you create 75 categories for your blog, there's absolutely no way you can possibly put them into a menu without it being overwhelming.

Even if you nest the menu items, it's still going to end up being a mess, and you're not really helping your readers by getting that specific.

Instead, shoot for about 3 to 5 categories for your entire blog, and if something is close, just stick it in the category that makes the most sense.

"Wouldn't it be so much easier if there were only three kinds of toothpaste?"

This way, when a user takes a look at your main menu, or at least the categories that you add to your menu, they only see a couple of choices, and it makes the process really easy.

Think about buying toothpaste. When you walk down the aisle, there has to be about 50 different kinds of toothpaste down there. Wouldn't it be nice if there was just maybe two or three? It would sure make the decision process easier, and it would also help you get where you're going in less time.

Your blog navigation menu needs to work the same way, and give people a small handful of choices to get where they need to go.

I recommend that you shoot for about five spaces total, which will give you plenty of room if you think about what to put in each one of those spaces.

Anything that's a sub point of another topic or category can be nested beneath your main five, but your main menu really shouldn't have very many choices.

The less choices you give your readers, the more likely they will pick one of those choices. Take a look at all the pages you have right now, and start organizing them into stacks. This means figure out the ones that are kind of related, because there's a little trick to creating menus coming up that you'll really like.

Nest Less Important Menu Items

Once you organize your pages into stacks, you can start doing something called nesting menu items.

This is where you hover over or click on one of your main five menu sections, and it creates a small pop-up below with the nested sections.

Let's say you have a website about woodworking, and you deal in three main branches. Those main branches are woodworking projects, woodworking tips, and woodworking tutorials.

"Nest smaller topic items inside a larger heading to simplify the main menu but still offer choice"

In this situation, create a main menu item named woodworking, and then nest all three category names underneath. This way, when the user hovers over woodworking, the menu pops out to show them the three main branches that you cover. Now, they can refine their click based on exactly what they're looking for.

You can also do this with all of your disclaimers, terms of service, and other necessary site documents to keep you legal.

A really great heading for this is simply the word legal, and then underneath you can have all of the other pages pop out so that way someone who is looking for your privacy policy can easily find it in that section of the menu.

"One of the most frustrating things you will ever encounter is a website that is difficult to navigate."

Just like you don't want your menu to be super cluttered, you also don't want your nested items to be gigantic either.

It's a good idea to limit these to about five as well, that way each of your five main menu items as 3 to 5 small choices right below it.

One of the most frustrating things that you will ever encounter is a website that's difficult to navigate through. After spending a couple of minutes looking for a particular section, and not finding it, it can become upsetting, and then you just leave.

You definitely don't want to provide this experience

for your readers. Instead, opt for a menu that makes a lot of sense, and that gets your readers to the places they need to go.

Once you have a little traffic, and you understand the choices of your readers, and more importantly the desires of your readers, you can adjust your menus to make sure that the majority of people coming to your site have easy access to the sections they are looking for.

Make changes on a small scale first, then make sure that everything that used to be in the menu is still discoverable in there somewhere.

One of the things you want to be careful about is changing your menu so often that people who regularly return to your site have a difficult time finding things.

As long as the menu still makes sense though, you can usually get away with just about any changes you look to make.

No Home on Menu

I'll save you one spot right now with a little tip that is not super obvious right in the beginning. On nearly every modern website, the site name, logo, or both will link to the

"Don't put a Home button on your menu."

homepage. This is a very common thing now and is expected when you click on the name of the logo.

What's the good news for you? Well, that means you don't have to waste one of your five main menu slots on a home button. That's right, if you have a home button in your menu right now you can completely remove it and it won't have any effect on the overwhelming majority of your readers.

Now, you have five menu slots that will serve you really well, as long as you get a little bit of organization, and you plan for those slots.

Use the Menu Ends Effectively

One of the things to pay attention to when designing your menu is the two items that you put on the far ends. No matter which way you arrange your five options, there will be one that's all the way on the left, and there will be one that's all the way on the right.

"The position on the left is going to be the most visible part of your menu."

Of all the different areas of your menu, these two are the ones to pay attention to.

When you glance at a menu on a website, you read from left to right, just like reading a book. The position on the left is going to be the most visible out of everything in your menu.

If you have a very important page, or page that you want as many people as possible to see when they check out your menu, then put it in the position all the way to the left.

The other important position is the one that's all the way on the right. This is the end of the menu, so this section will be memorable as well, but not nearly as much as the position all the way on the left.

If you put a couple of good pages in these places, and your menu text is enticing, you'll get a lot more clicks than burying something in the middle.

Shorten Individual Menu Names

Your menu is only going to be so wide, so you are going to have to use little tricks to make sure that all of your different menu items fit in that space. One of the things you can do is alter the names of the different pages and posts so that when they fit.

WordPress makes this really easy, and it's right inside of the menu editor.

All you need to do is look at the section where it

shows you what the title will look like on the actual menu, and change the text. This is great for pages and posts that have long titles, because one or two of these can kill your entire menu if you're not careful.

You can also do little tricks to shorten very common menu items

"One long title can kill your menu."

that people just know and understand. For example, you don't need to put the words about me, or about with your business name. All you need to do is use the word about, and anyone looking at your menu is going to know exactly what that page is about.

The same goes for contact instead of contact me or contact my business. The single word contact is all you need.

Now, take a look at all the different pages, and the items that you need to include in your menu. Think of a simple and short way to change the name so that way it makes sense, but makes your menu as small as possible. Even though you have five or so spaces, you don't need to have them be super wide. If you have a very tight menu with five single words for each one of your categories, that can look very clean and inviting.

Make Site Navigation Easy

Of all the things that you do when you design the layout of your site, the big theme that you want to keep in mind is making the navigation as easy as possible.

If you don't have a rule for something, just apply this one. Does this make the navigation easy, or difficult? If it's easy, then go ahead and include it, but if it's difficult, you need to come up with a different solution.

If you keep your categories simple, and you keep your design clean, you pretty much won't ever have to worry about people getting lost on your site. The average reader will be able to figure their way around very quickly, and you won't lose people because they can't find things that used to be able to find.

One of the best things that you can do is think about helping your readers whenever you

"Think about helping your readers whenever you make a navigation change."

make any design or navigation changes on your site. There is however one thing that you can do without even thinking, and that's adding a search bar.

Add a Search Bar

The search bar is a common feature on nearly all websites, and that's thanks to the search engine. You don't even need to tell people what to do with the search bar on your site, all you need to do is display it, and they will know exactly how to use it.

This is great, because if you accidentally end up moving a piece of content that someone really likes, they can go right to the search bar and type in enough of the name that they will still be able to find it.

This is a simple thing that you can do to make your website easier to navigate, and it's super helpful on websites that have a lot of posts and pages.

Once you start getting over 100 posts, finding things by scrolling can get pretty miserable. Instead of asking your readers to scroll endlessly, just include a search bar, because even if they don't know the exact name, the can get close enough that the search bar will still return the result they are looking for.

You can also use multiple search bars, and you are definitely not restricted to putting them in just one place.

You can have search bar right at the top of your site, in the header, in a sidebar, and in the footer. You can also do any combination of these, and don't feel like you're overdoing it. Giving your user the ability to search for what they are looking for is a huge benefit to them, and providing enough search bars that they can find one in a pinch is also a good service.

"Giving your readers the ability to search on their own is a huge benefit to them."

If you've ever done any type of woodworking, you know how easy it is to lose your tape measure. On the outside, you wouldn't think that a person wouldn't need more than one tape measure in order to build a woodworking project. However, a tape measure just disappears the moment you need to use it.

For this reason, I have about five or six tape measures floating around in my shop. This way, pretty much no matter where I am, there is always a tape measure within my line of sight.

Just as having multiple tape measures might sound

silly on the outside, and having multiple search bar sounds about the same, the moment your user needs one of these and finds it quickly the whole process becomes worth it.

Another good trick to including the search bar is to include it in a place that will always be on every single page, no matter where your user goes.

A good candidate is your sidebar, and your header. Both of these things materialize on every single page unless you disable them, so you can be assured that no matter where your reader is on your site, that they will have search bars available to them.

Tips and Tricks for Design and Navigation

Here are a few tips and tricks for the design and navigation of your site that can help you make a great looking blog that's easy to get around in:

- Be as clean as possible in your design, and understand that a simple design done really well is far better than a complex design executed poorly.

- Pick a good color scheme for your website, and if you can't think of anything immediately, just go with black and white, because it goes with everything.

- Including very simple menu that you have on all of your pages, and try to include no more than five different choices on the main menu.

- If you have a lot of categories on your website, consider condensing them down to 3 to 5. This way, it will be a lot less confusing to your reader.

- Strategically place your search bars so that way there is always one available when your readers need to find a particular piece of content on your blog.

Chapter Five

Calls to Action and Links

Any time you ask your readers to click on something, this is a call to action. It might not outright scream to be clicked on, but even a simple text link is a call to action asking for the click.

When you think about it, there are a lot of different things on your website that are all competing for the attention of your reader. These are not limited to just the words that are on the page. There are images, quotes, links, advertisements, and many other elements that are all begging for some sort of action from your reader.

Understanding this, it's easy to see how people get out of hand with their website very

"It's easy to see how people get out of hand with their calls to action when you see how easy it is to add them."

quickly, because it's really easy to add these elements. Instead of overloading your site, keep it simple, and provide only the most relevant links and calls to action possible.

This way, not only will you have a higher chance of getting the user to take action, they will be happier with where it takes them.

This helps develop trust, and send signals to your readers that you really care about them.

Ask Small in the Beginning

When it comes to selling, or asking your readers to do pretty much anything, it's best to ask small in the beginning. This means you don't want to start off your blog post by asking your reader to go somewhere else or trying to hard sell them.

"In the beginning, your readers have no idea who you are, and they don't trust you."

Instead, you want to start out small.

In the beginning, your readers absolutely no idea who you are, and they don't trust you. Since they don't know you and they don't trust you, the odds of you getting them to buy something right away are extraordinarily low.

If you waste your products right at the top of your posts, unless it's an extremely soft sell for people who have been to your site a bunch of times before, you're going to lose out on a lot of sales.

Also, people might think your site is a taking site instead of giving site, and that can turn them off right away.

It's easy to tell right away if you're on a website that just wants your money. Also, it's easy to tell when you're on a website that wants to help you succeed.

The beauty and the craft of designing a blog is in showing people that you do want them to be successful, but also selling in a way that's not confrontational, and almost effortless.

This is how you make sure that your website is viewed as a giving site and a supportive site.

One of the best ways to do this is to ask small in the beginning. An example of a small ask is offering someone a freebie. While giving away something doesn't immediately sound like asking for something, you are asking for their permission to share something, and you still do need their approval.

The reason this is considered a small ask is that it's much easier to ask someone to give them something than it is to ask them to give something to you. The beauty of a freebie is that it starts to build trust, because you're the first person to give something.

> *"A freebie starts to build trust because you are the first person to give something."*

If that freebie is filled with excellent information, and it helps them be successful, you may be rewarded by them returning to your site and purchasing from you in the future.

You also make sure to put your website information in that freebie so that they can click on it any time they want to come back and get more.

With modern downloadable files, it's very easy to embed a link that launches their Internet browser and puts them right back on your site. This is a way to get your readers back when they are enjoying their freebie.

Another small ask is to offer to answer questions that they might have about the topic, or to offer to deliver tips or tricks in their email.

These goals help you and your reader, because it opens up a line of communication to the people that consume your content, and it allows them the opportunity to interact with you.

When someone signs up to receive free tips every month, they are giving you their email address, and giving you permission to be in their inbox at a certain interval. Building an email list with a small ask where your reader allows you to give them something is a good way of softly adding people to your list.

When you deliver what you promised, you end up building trust, and those readers will come back much more often.

Ask Big in the End

When you do ask for a sale, it's best to do this closer to the end of your post. There are many reasons for this, but the main reason is that you have more trust at the end than you have at the beginning.

Especially if you write long and detailed content, that's full of a lot of amazing ideas, and teaches people how to be successful at something, they might spend 10 minutes or half an hour on your page. That's a very long time, and in Internet minutes, almost like dog years, that's an eternity.

"You have more trust at the end than you do at the beginning."

By the time someone has spent a half an hour with you, and you've been carefully and thoroughly educating them about the topic, they start to see you as an authority. Your readers will look to you as an expert, especially if they have read good material for the last half hour.

At this point, many of your readers will already be primed to take the next step. This is where coming in and offering a paid solution to one of their problems can actually work out in everyone's favor.

The customer you are selling to definitely gets more benefit than you, because they will have a solution to their problem, or a product that they will really enjoy. Since the products are related to the post, it's a natural extension of something they already like, or a problem that they already need to solve.

You also benefit far more at this point in the relationship, because you have a much better opportunity of selling this product then you would if you tried to sell at the very top of the post.

After all, you haven't built any kind of relationship at all in the beginning, you only just started to build one near the end.

This would be like going on a date with somebody that you've never met, and asking them to marry you before you've even shaken their hand. The odds of that happening are extremely low, and you're definitely not going to get a lot of buyers.

Also, you don't have to wait until the very end before you start planting the seeds, and selling. You can start soft selling your products or services in around the last half to the last third of the post.

This will get people primed for the idea that you do have other solutions besides just your blog post, and those are available for people who want to take the next step.

By the time someone sticks with you all the way to the end of your post, especially if you write in a conversational tone that's like speaking to a friend that you've known for years, you are going to have built up quite a good relationship in a very short amount of time.

This is when you ask for the sale. Not only will you have a better chance of selling your product or service, your customer will believe in you more at this point, and they will have a better chance of enjoying it.

Internal Links

The internal links of your site are mini calls to action to get people to look at additional pieces of content that exist on your site. It's important when you include your internal links that they are all relevant to the area in which you include them.

"Don't link to a post about pinewood derby cars in a post about chocolate chip cookies."

This means even if you have the most amazing article on building a pinewood derby car, you don't want to link to it in a post about chocolate chip cookies.

In fact, you probably don't even want to have those

two things together on the same website because I can't even think of a way that they are related, other than possibly enjoying some chocolate chip cookies after winning a pinewood derby race.

Even though that's an extreme example, there are times when you'll see links like this on other websites and you'll notice that they are out of place. If this isn't something that you're consciously doing on your website, you can probably go back now and find some links that don't exactly make perfect sense either.

For example, if you are writing a post about composting, and you've already written a lot of content about gardening, you probably still want to focus your internal links on other aspects of composting, even though the two are still related.

However, if you have nothing else at this point, you can include some internal links that are a little bit looser in their relation until you build up a larger volume of content. Then, you can just go back and link to things that are more relevant.

Your internal links are an opportunity for you to provide additional content for your readers without having to supply all of that content on the main page.

> *"A well placed set of internal links functions almost like those old make your own mystery books."*

This lets you keep your post focused on the main topic, but you can still include branches of that topic if your readers want to go down a particular path.

A well-placed series of internal links almost functions like one of those old make your own mystery books that you might have read as a kid.

Do you remember those books where you read a few pages and then you have a choice of what you want the hero to do? Then, for each decision you need to turn to a different page? This is what links do for your blog posts. It gives readers a chance to make their own story out of your content.

One of the most amazing things that will happen to you over time and as you build up a healthy number of blog posts, is that your internal link search will become much better.

"As you build up your content, your internal link opportunities will become better and more specific."

When you write a paragraph about a certain topic, and you want to include an internal link, you'll be able to search with a keyword from that topic, and it will return several results for related posts that you already written.

This happens once you have enough material and you've covered lots of different topics.

The beauty at this stage of blogging is that you can include a relevant internal link in just about every subsection of your post to take the readers farther on that particular aspect of the journey. It's a great experience for your reader, because if they have questions at any stage of your post, there's a supplemental post to help explain things further.

In the beginning, focus on linking to other pages on your own site that make sense and help elevate your current post. I recommend writing about five posts and then going back and interlinking them all where it makes sense.

From there, you should have enough material to add a least one or two relevant internal links to every post you write going forward. This number will increase over time of course as you build up a larger volume of content. However, in the beginning this is plenty.

External Links

External links are a bit misunderstood when it comes to writing blog posts. The obvious problem with an external link is that you're sending your readers to another website. You spend all this time trying to build traffic, and then you just go and send it to somebody else.

"Relevant external links show your readers that you love them enough to let them go."

While it might sound like that's what you're doing on the surface, it's really not. When you provide a relevant external link, you show your audience that you love them enough to give them the information they need to be successful, even though it's not on your own website.

This is an amazing act of generosity, because it's really easy to be selfish and just keep people on your own website, especially since you fought so hard to get them there.

Your readers will appreciate external links when they add value, and they help them solve their problems.

Most people are only going to be on your website for about one page anyway, so the odds of you keeping them forever are very low. Since they are leaving anyway, you might as well send them in the right direction.

Also, external links can be used to verify stats and facts that you put in your posts.

Unless you are an expert on population statistics, you should include a citation and a relevant link to the source whenever you quote population statistics. The same goes if you are quoting statistics from any other industry. It's just a good idea to show that you're not making this stuff up.

Even the search engines appreciate this type of behavior, because it shows that you're not all about you, and that you're willing to provide proof of what you're saying.

If your readers were to click on any of these sources and find out that you were full of crap, they would stop coming to your website. This means you have a vested interest in displaying the truth.

"It's likely that you are only one small part of a long series of searches on a particular topic."

Another thing that external links do is help predict the next step for your readers, which is also something that the search engines like.

Many searchers use several different terms at different times during the process in order to refine and figure out exactly how to solve their problem. You might only be one small segment of this search behavior.

If you can help your reader advance to the next stage without going back to the search engine and picking a different result for the same search term, you send a signal to the search engines that you gave them the answer they were looking for.

This is an excellent signal, because it verifies that

you were a good search result for that particular keyword or key phrase. If you continue to do this, your post will be pushed further up in the rankings for that term.

Even though external links are important, you don't have to go nuts with them. Just include them when they make sense, and don't feel like you need to include an external link in every single one of your posts. Include them when you need them, and then think about doing one more thing on your own site afterwards.

"Even though external links are important, you don't have to go nuts with them."

If the content you are linking to is something that you can create yourself, and is part of your field of expertise, consider generating a similar piece of content that fills the same information gap on your own site.

At that point, you can replace the external link

within internal link, and still provide people with the same information, but keep the traffic yourself.

You won't be able to do this with everything of course. When it comes to linking to tools, or complex web pages, you may not have the capability to produce this kind of work yourself.

You may also not have the expertise or the knowledge. That's okay, just apply the idea to stuff that you know really well. Everything else can remain an external link.

Make Posts Easy to Link To

On the subject of links, it's also really important that you make your post easy to link to. Inbound links are one of the biggest signals to the search engines that you've created good content. After all, people won't willingly link to crappy content.

Since most of your readers are going to be average people, not super amazing bloggers like yourself, you need to provide a way to link to your post really easily.

The best way to do this is with social share buttons that you can find as a WordPress *"The easier you make it for people to do what you want them to do, the more often they will do it."* plug-in. You can use a free version in the beginning, but eventually you want to settle on one plug-in that does what you need, even if you have to pay a little bit for it.

This plug-in will allow you to have your readers share your post and link to it with a single click instead of having to copy the URL and do a lot of other work to make that happen.

The easier you make it for people to do what you want them to do, the more often they will do it. Social share buttons are just one example of this phenomenon. When you put the buttons on your site, you just might be surprised at how often people will use them.

Though inbound links from social media aren't as strong as inbound links from another website, giving your readers the ability to share your post is a great way to help you increase your site traffic.

When someone shares your content, they tend to share it with their friends, or in a group of like-minded individuals. This means if one reader likes your content enough to share it, odds are the people they are sharing it with will like it to.

The bottom line is that the more people who share your content and link to your site from either their website or their social media profiles, the more traffic you are going to get and the more favorable you appear in the eyes of the search engines.

When people vote for you by sharing your content without being paid, or told to do so, it's a huge signal for everyone.

You should pay attention to this signal too, because the types of content on your site that are shared the most is the way your readers vote for the content that they enjoy the most.

If you provide supporting articles and posts that enhance those that are already being shared at a higher velocity, you can be nearly sure that your readers will also like that content.

"Your readers vote for their favorite content on your site by how often they share certain posts."

This is an easy way to branch from one topic to the next. Not only will it be something that you have experience with, but it will also be something that your audience has demonstrated that they like.

That's a win for everyone.

Leave Text Links Blue

This is going to be about the easiest of all the ideas in this book, because if you do it right, it actually involves you doing nothing.

"Any underlined links in a different color than blue look suspicious to your readers."

Whatever you do with the colors on your website, even though I advise you to leave them black and white like every other website in the world, you definitely don't want to touch your link colors.

The Internet has been around long enough to program people that blue text with a blue underline is a link. People have also used the Internet long enough to know that any other color of underlined text and words is suspicious.

The very last thing you want to do when you are asking your readers to click on a link is make them suspicious of it in any way.

Believe it or not, people are still a little bit afraid of their computers. When you present a suspicious looking link, the natural inclination in most people is not to click on it. Since links are supposed to be blue, when you provide green or orange links, they do stand out, which is great, but they sometimes stand out for a bad reason.

"People are still a little bit afraid of their computers."

Any link color other than blue, or purple when the link has already been visited draws suspicion.

Instead of wasting time changing your link color, and wondering why people aren't clicking on them at all, just leave your in text links blue like every other website on the planet. This makes them very familiar, and it won't scare away your readers when they want to click.

The only exception to this rule is if you want to try a different color link text in your calls to action. Adds, and calls to action need to look different many times in order to be effective. One of the ways that you can play around with this effectiveness is to see if a different color link text gets you more clicks in that particular ad or call to action.

The links that are found inside of your paragraphs however need to remain blue, because that's what people expect, and it will help make sure that they're not afraid of clicking.

Use Colored Text in CTAs

As far as the colored text goes in your calls to action, you should definitely try different things in the beginning, just to see what resonates with your readers, and if you can draw a few more clicks by making the text more obvious.

If you like more subtle calls to action, and you don't like to include a banner, or an image, or anything that really resembles an ad, you can differentiate your calls to action by just changing the text color for the link.

This is pretty effective when you use a very short sentence asking your reader to take

"If you leave your call to action link blue, you might risk it not being noticed as much."

some sort of action. It may be something as simple as click for free tips in orange text that links to a newsletter sign-up.

In some cases, if you leave this as the standard blue text, and you leave it the same size, you might run the risk of it not being noticed.

However, when you combine a loud color with a subtle call to action, sometimes you can mix up the secret sauce it takes to get people to take action in large numbers.

Add Buttons to CTAs

People love buttons. Even more so, people love pushing buttons. The only thing that gets clicks more than a link is a button, and if you are generating your own calls to action, consider including a button for the action instead of a link.

"When you push a button, you really feel like you've taken an acton."

Though the button does the exact same thing as a link, psychologically it's a little bit different for your reader. When you push a button, you really feel like you've taken an action. A link is just a click, and you're used to clicking on things anyway.

Buttons are different.

Unless you're going to learn how to write HTML and CSS by hand, I recommend that you just pick up a lightweight plug-in that allows you to insert buttons wherever you want. Most of these are free, and they'll give you several different styles button and you can pick lots of different colors and sizes. You can also add little icons to the buttons sometimes, and that's fun too.

When you include a button on your call to action, you could end up getting more clicks simply because the call to action is more visible.

"Text surrounded by text tends to disappear."

Text surrounded by text tends to disappear. If you add a button below that text, you can combine a subtle call to action with a button that's a little bit louder.

Again, this is a good blend because it ensures that people see your message, but delivers it in a way that doesn't seem forceful or or rude.

Again, people become suspicious of things that they don't understand or that they don't trust. Keep your calls to action subtle but obvious, and you can achieve a good blend of offering the sale, but not shoving it down anyone's throat.

Give Away a Freebie

One of the smartest things that you can do on your site is give away a freebie.

It's even better if you can give away several freebies, and because you have your own blog, you can do it in a number of different ways.

The most common way is to ask for an email address in order to receive the goodies, but I think that's a bad idea.

Most people who exchange their email address for a free download will remove themselves from your mailing list the second after they get the download.

Yep, you read that right.

There is no honor on the internet. People will download your freebie, and use the email it came in to unsubscribe from your list.

All this does is make it look like you're sending spam emails, and that can cause you problems down the road with using bulk email systems. Besides, someone that's just into your email newsletter because they're going to get something for free is not the type of person you want on your list.

> *"There is no honor on the internet. People will download your freebie and use the email it came in to unsubscribe from your list."*

Instead, give the freebie away completely for free, which means you just host the file on your site, and anyone can download it without any type of barriers in their way.

This is really the definition of free anyway, because when you give someone an email address, sure you didn't give them any money, but you still had to give them something in order to receive something for free. That just doesn't make sense, because free means I don't have to give anything, including my email address.

"Inside that freebie, include a way to restart the relationship if the reader decides they need you again."

The great thing about free downloads is that you can very easily showcase your ability to teach and help, and deliver it in a way that your reader gets to keep it forever. Inside of that content, you include a way to contact you, and a way to restart that relationship should the person ever decide to in the future.

Most of the people that take your downloads will never come back, but that's okay. It's not worth chasing after people that don't want to be a part of your world. There are plenty that do, and those are the ones that you need to love.

Offering your downloads completely for free, and

without any type of barriers is still something that will set you apart in the blogging world.

People are used to having to give in order to get, so when you provide something completely for free, it really starts to build that trust between you and your readers.

"The easiest freebie is a download, because you only have to create it once and it costs nothing to give away."

There are a lot of different things that you can do as a freebie. The easiest is some sort of a download, because it's something that you don't have to pay for, and you only need to make once. You can literally spend a couple hours working on a nice download and tons of people can enjoy it without it costing you one cent.

The type of download that you offer really depends on your niche, but just about any topic can use something like a quick start guide, a tools list, a set of great tips, or some method of tracking progress.

For example, if you're in the composting niche, a Quick Start Guide to Composting is a perfect free giveaway. It targets beginners, and it gives them a quick win thanks to your website.

"Giving a beginner a win makes you the hero, and they will remember that when it comes time to buy."

Another good example would be the ultimate guitar making tool list, which shows new guitar makers the tools that they'll need to build their own guitar. Again, this is targeted towards beginners, but it's one of the biggest frustrations that they have, and you'll be the one to alleviate it for them.

That makes you the hero, and your readers will remember that when it comes time to buy.

Add Elements With Hooks

One of the amazing things that lots of web page

builders and themes do is they allow you to use something called hooks. This is where you get to inject a piece of content in a certain part of your site, and you have a lot of control over the placement of this insertion.

GeneratePress makes this very easy, and they include many different hook locations within your pages and posts. They allow you to add something globally, no matter how many pages you have on your site with just a few clicks. This is very helpful for your calls to action and for sharing when you have a new product.

Imagine you have a site that has 500 pages. If you wanted to add something above every post that talks about your new book coming out, you would have to go into every single post, open them up one at a time, and paste that information at the top. You would then have to save the post, exit, and open another.

Even if you were able to go through this entire

process in 30 seconds per post, you're still looking at about four hours worth of work to make one change globally. In contrast, you paste the information into your hook, and your theme puts it on every single page no matter what.

"You can use hooks to display your own calls to action and they can populate on all pages just by editing one thing."

You can also limit the location and the placement through the settings, which is nice if you want to do category specific hooks.

Let's say you've written a few different books, and each one of them has to do with one of the categories on your site. You can create a hook that displays a nice picture of your book, with a call to action, and it could show up with the right book in the right category no matter which page your reader visits.

Pretty cool.

This is also useful for adding different elements that work with short codes, or that can be populated after the post, like a related posts section.

All you need to do is add this little bit of code to your hook, place it after your post, and every

"Lots of bloggers use hooks to run ads for their own products."

single post on your site will have the content when it loads.

Many bloggers use these elements to run their own ads for their own products. They also use them to place different elements globally on the site that aren't as easy to place by hand.

For example, you can put an author bio picture right underneath the title of all of your posts. This way, your readers can get to know what you look like, and start building a personal relationship.

The other beautiful part about using hooks is that they are so easy to replace. You might have a hook near the top of your site that displays news or information, and shares what's going on with your blog. As the news changes, which is the nature of news, all you need to do is go in and change what the hook says, and it will change across the entire site.

The only place were hooks fall short is that they don't allow you to place elements within your body content. For example, you can't place a hook five paragraphs into every single post. This is a job for a different tool, and that's coming up.

Ad Inserter for In-Content Ads

Let's say you want to add a specific piece of content within the main body area of your post. This could be somewhere near the top, somewhere near the middle, or somewhere near the bottom. It doesn't really matter, as long as it's inside your paragraphs of body text.

Hooks will not work for this purpose, so you need to use a different tool. The easiest and the best tool to use is called Ad Inserter, which is a free plug-in that you can download while inside of WordPress.

All you need to do is download and install the program, and it offers a lot of different options for inserting different bits of content in your posts.

At first, you're going to have to play around with the user interface, just to get an idea of how to make everything work.

However, you can inject content in a lot of different ways, and there are so many different tricks for including, excluding, and placing the injections that you really have a ton of control.

You can include posts, exclude posts, include categories, exclude categories, and you can even specify how many paragraphs should go by before the element is inserted.

You can also repeat the same element after a certain number of additional paragraphs, so you can insert the same thing multiple times if you want.

"After a while, if you don't update your ads, your readers won't even see them anymore."

It's a lot of control, and it gives you the ability to update the calls to action on your site regularly, which is one of the secrets to keeping them fresh.

People just get immune to your ads. After a while, your readers won't even see them anymore. In order to keep selling, you're going to have to freshen up your look, and swap out your calls to action to keep them effective.

Ad Inserter makes this incredibly easy, because all you need to do is change the information that gets inserted into your posts, and just like that, the content changes across your entire site.

If you ever need to turn one of these insertions off,

all you need to do is go into the plug-in and pause that insertion. In just a few seconds and a couple clicks, it will no longer add that piece of content to your posts.

This is a great tool for directing people to a certain piece of content that's your bread-and-butter or where you get the highest conversion. After a few paragraphs in each post you can include a call to action that helps people with their biggest problem, or at least the biggest problem that you know of for people interested in your niche.

A lot of people that see that call to action will take action upon it, because if they're already searching for the content you are creating, odds are they are one of the people that has the most common problem in that niche.

You can be the one to solve their problem, which means an insertion like this can be really powerful.

Getting people to take action on your site also

reduces your bounce rate, and sends a signal to the search engines that people like your content.

Besides, when you genuinely give people a win, they start to naturally behave in a way that helps you. This includes sharing your content, visiting more of your posts, lingering on your site longer, and eventually buying from you.

Ad Inserter will also save you a lot of time. If you had to manually place a call to action near your last few paragraphs in every post, it could take you a very long time.

If you have a large site, it can take hours or even days to do. Then, a few weeks after you're done, you'll probably have to change that content again to keep it fresh.

Instead of wasting all that time, just let a plug-in do the work for you. This way, you only have to come up with the information one time, and add it to your site one time.

After that, the plug-in does all of the work, and that's fantastic.

Tips and Tricks for CTAs and Links

Here are some tips and tricks for your calls to action and links that can help you make these as effective as possible:

- Everything that you placed on your site that can be clicked on can be considered a call to action, even the most basic of links.

- Include internal links on your site to content that enriches and expands the section in which you include the link. Make sure that it's relevant, and that it adds to the experience.

- Include external links where they make sense, and to give users a complete solution when they visit your post.

- Don't change your link color for your in text links, however you can experiment with color when it comes to your calls to action.

- When you have to make big insertions on your site, use hooks, or use a plug-in like Ad Inserter that way you don't have to manually add the content to every single post.

Chapter Six

Headers and Footers

When it comes to your headers and your footers, there are a few things that can help you to create a blog post that doesn't distract the reader from your main content.

Your header is a great place to announce the name of your blog, and add a short tagline that helps people immediately understand what your website is about. Your footer is great for closing things out with some good calls to action and some resources to be able to take the next step.

There are some things you can do to ensure that your headers and footers function in the way that they should, and they contribute to the overall quality of your post.

"In general, make your header quick and your footer more detailed."

Things like using smaller headers, and packing your footer with some awesome goodies are great ways to maximize both of these areas on your website.

In general, you want to make your header quick and your foot or more detailed. This way, you don't distract people with your header, but you offer a lot of value in your footer for the people who make it all the way to the bottom.

Ask small in the beginning, and ask big in the end.

This is a good way to look at your header and your footer respectively.

Use Small Headers

The first thing about your headers is that I recommend you keep it as small as possible while still allowing room to show your logo and your tagline.

It's important that your readers start getting familiar with your name and your logo.

It's also important that they're able to quickly scan your tagline and understand exactly what type of blog you're running.

In most cases, this is going to be the first impression that anyone landing on your side is going to encounter.

If you have a simple but effective header, you can show your readers everything they need to know about you and your site in a very small amount of space.

Anything that you can do to increase familiarity and trust is a welcome addition to your website. When someone selects a random search result, they're hoping they're going to find the right answer.

When they land on your site for the first time and immediately see something comforting, it increases their trust level ever so slightly.

"Anything you can do to increase familiarity and trust is a welcome addition to your website."

This is great, because it means you are taking steps right away to help your reader feel like they are in the right place, and they can trust you enough to scroll down and find the right answer.

That's really what it's all about. It's building trust every step of the way so your reader continues to go through your website without anything startling them or making them feel suspicious.

I recommend that you make a small header that includes your site name, logo if you have one, and tagline. Make it as short as possible, and as long as it's easy to read, then it's not too long.

Once you have it in place, the other thing that you'll notice is that your above the fold content area actually starts to fill with real content. This means your header won't take up the entire first screen, and you'll actually get your reader to see more right away.

This is fantastic, because it can help with your above the fold content, and the first impression that your reader has of your site.

Footers Can be Larger

When it comes to the footer on your website, you can be as large or a small as you want. The footer is the section at the very bottom of every single page, and it takes a while for your user to get all the way down there.

"Footers can be big because they are at the end and you don't have to scroll past it to get to the main content."

Due to it taking a while to get all the way to the bottom, it generally means that the reader has spent a lot of time on your site, and also got some value from it.

If you create a larger footer, you can provide them even more value and hopefully rescue them before they exit and go somewhere else.

Another reason your footer can be so big is that you don't have to worry about scrolling past it in order to get to your content.

The header is kind of in the way, because it's the first thing that populates on your site. The footer on the other hand is the last thing, so you can make this as large as you want.

Don't go nuts with your footer, but make it as big as you need to in order to include a lot of great content that the user may not have directly landed upon. This is a good place for some of your best performing posts that appeal to the widest range of your audience.

This is one last chance to hook your reader on something else that you created, so the more opportunities you give that footer, the better chance it will have at getting your reader on to another article.

Simple Headers Load Faster

Something really nice to mention about simple headers is that they load much faster than complex headers.

The more you cram into that header, and the more intense you make it, the longer it's going to take to load. When you think about it, there's already a lot of stuff loading right away in the beginning, so you really don't need to overload it anymore than it already is.

When you put an image in your header, if that's your plan, make sure that it is the smallest and the lightest file size that you can possibly use that doesn't look crappy.

"If you use an image in your header, make sure it's the lightest file you can possibly create that doesn't look crappy."

Make sure the image doesn't look pixelated, or poorly taken, and keep reducing the quality until you get it as small as possible.

Images are one of your site elements that take the longest to load. If you are going to have an image in the header, it definitely needs to be light and easy loading in order to ensure a good user experience.

Keeping your header light also includes keeping a lot of random text out of there. You don't need to explain a bunch of stuff in your header, that's actually better done in a hook or an ad insertion on every post. Your header needs to load fast, and be light weight in order for your post to work most effectively.

Make Your Header Easy to Understand

Above all else, your header needs to be easy to understand. If you follow the template that I've given you already, can you include your name, logo, and tagline, that should be sufficient that your site header is easy to interpret.

Something you can do to test your header is just ask a friend who doesn't really have much experience in your genre to take a look at it.

Have them read your name and tagline, and then

tell you what the website is about. They should be able to do it just from that small amount of information and nothing else.

"A stranger should be able to tell you exactly what your site is about from your title and tagline."

If they can't, and your niche isn't super obscure to the point where there's only two people on the planet that know about it, you need to make some adjustments. It's important that your website is easy to understand. Anything that raises the difficulty level will scare away your readers.

Going back to the very beginning of the book, in everything you do, ask if this makes an easy experience for the reader.

Comprehension makes things easy, so the more understandable the content in your header, the easier it's going to be for your reader to continue and understand what they're about to consume.

Resist the urge to be cheeky or subversive in your header. Just tell people exactly where they are and what to expect. This is the easiest way to make your header understandable, and in turn make your website understandable.

Remove Headers on Sales Pages

When it comes to the pages that you use to sell, the lower the number of calls to action the better.

In fact, you may only want to put one or two possible options on a page like that. This way, you funnel the reader exactly towards the action that you want them to take.

One thing that you can do with your site design is to remove your header and much of the menu content from your sales pages.

This is really effective on a landing page that comes

from an ad. When you're paying for the traffic, you definitely want to convert as many of those people as possible.

Every element that you have on your website is a distraction, and it's own call to action. If you give your reader too many places to click, you run the risk of the reader clicking on something that you don't really want them to.

A strategy you can try if you like is removing the header from these kinds of pages. Try it out, and see if you get a better conversion from the traffic.

If you have no traffic at this point, you can't test it, but you can try it. See if you like a cleaner sales page, or page where people need to take action in a way that results in furthering the sales process.

You are not hurting or tricking your readers when you do this. You are helping them make a good decision and not cluttering up the screen with random choices.

If you have believe in your product, and you feel like it makes a big difference in the lives of your readers, there is nothing wrong with wanting them to take action to own it.

If you feel like asking for the sale is too pushy, that's fine. Just remember that it's easy

"It's easy to confuse lack of faith in your product as being push with the sale."

to confuse lack of faith in your product with being pushy. Make sure you fully believe in your product before you label trying to make the sale as pushy.

People that do not believe in their products tend to feel like even asking for the sale is pushy, and that's definitely not the case with a great product.

After all, why wouldn't you want the lives of your readers to be better?

If you don't believe in your product enough to ask for the sale, you need a better product, and you owe it to your readers to make one.

Do this, and you will find it very easy to make people's lives better with your blog and your products.

Use Footers for Calls to Action

Your footer is a great place for a call to action. If you think about it, when a user makes it all the way to the bottom of your website, the very last thing that they are going to encounter is your footer.

This is your very last chance to get them to do something, and take action.

Like most websites, you've probably had several calls to action up to this point. By the time someone reaches your footer, they will have likely gone through many different attempts at getting them to click on something or another.

Even though your efforts may have not worked out

up to this point, it's still important to think about somewhere to direct your reader now that they've trusted you enough to read all the way through your content and land at the bottom.

This call to action can be a little different than the others, and should be based on the behavior you anticipate.

"Someone who has consumed a lot of your content may be ready for something bigger once they reach the bottom of your post."

For example, someone who has consumed all of your content on that page and enjoyed it enough to stay there for a while might like something a little bit longer from you.

If the article that they've just read wasn't super long, maybe it's time to direct them to something that's more substantial, because they may be primed to consume a lot of your content now.

This is where something like an ultimate guide, a step-by-step tutorial, or a short course on how to do something may be appropriate. These are generally longer offerings, and they play really well to someone that already trust you enough to spend a lot of time on your site.

You may even decide to include links to some of your more popular content, or some of your downloads. It's likely that both of these are longer in nature, and they're really helpful. This is awesome, because the person that stuck with you to the end definitely doesn't want to be let down, especially after investing so much time in you.

Instead of letting them down, make sure that these links are some of your best, and that you direct these readers to content that will keep them on your website even longer.

Not only is this great for them, because they're obviously getting good information if they're sticking around, it's also great for you because they're spending so much time on the page.

The longer they stick around, the better your website looks. Also, the more they stick around, the more opportunities they have to land on one of your calls to action, and hopefully buy.

Your footer can also be very simple with just one very effective call to action, or perhaps a couple.

"Sometimes, being plain and simple and only offering one place to go is an effective option."

Sometimes, being very plain and simple and only offering your reader one place to go is the best route. If you've already spent a lot of your previous calls to action, it's a good idea to make this one different, and changing the format a little bit can help it stand out too.

If someone is made it all the way to the bottom and they've skipped all of your previous calls to action, asking again the same way may not necessarily be the best option.

It's true that people do need to be asked several times for the sale, but if you've already done that effectively throughout the post, this last link may be more effective if it were different.

It also may be more effective just offering more free content.

When a person is ready to buy from you, they will buy from you. Especially if they get to know you through your blog posts, develop some interest in you, and begin to trust you, the sales will come. If you have someone that's reluctant to buy right now, the best thing you can do is shower them with your free content and continue to help them.

This will do nothing but reinforce the bond between the two of you.

In contrast, if you run away after the sale isn't made, you leave a bad taste in the mouth of your reader that will likely prevent them from ever coming back. It's much better to have someone who might come back then someone who will never come back. This is where continuing to give even though you're not getting anything in return is a worthwhile investment.

Add Sections to the Footer

Another thing that's effective in your footer is adding sections. It's pretty simple to add two or three columns to your footer, and include a different section of content in each one of them.

For example, your first column can be your greatest hits. Then, your middle column might be some of your user requested content. Finally, your end column can be more nuts and bolts like search boxes, site maps, and general links that you would find in the main menu.

You could also separate your footer into a few different sections and make each one of them a call to action for your main categories. You can also turn these into really effective calls to action by changing the name of the categories to mirror the reader instead of the actual category.

"Nobody wants to be a beginner, so sometimes it's better received to offer to teach rather than call out your beignners."

For example, if you run a knitting site, and you have several different posts in a category for beginners, your call to action might be Let Me Teach You How to Knit.

This can be more effective than the phrase Beginning Knitting, because it tells the reader exactly what to expect and it's less offputting than accusing someone of being a beginner.

This is something we're all guilty of, and it's a shame. Nobody wants to be a beginner anymore, so sometimes it's better to offer to teach somebody then to outright call them a beginner. Even though everyone is a beginner in the beginning, and you need to absorb that entry-level content in order to advance, sometimes it's easy for people to skip over this section.

When you arrange your calls to action in the different sections of your footer, just think about what your readers would really like, and turn your categories into a representation of that. This way, when they get to the bottom, they'll go to one of your few main categories based on what they like the most.

This is fantastic for you because you get to keep these readers on your website longer. It's also great for them because they'll get to go to exactly the type of content they are looking for, which means they'll spend even more time on your site.

The easier you make it for people to find what they need to find, even in your footer, the better.

Add Legal Stuff to Footer

The footer is also a good opportunity to reiterate the legal content that you have on your website. On any website, you'll have certain legal documents like a privacy policy, disclaimer, and data rights. Each of these is important to be readily available for your readers, and not difficult to find.

One of the ways to make these documents easy to find is to place them in multiple locations on each page. You should already have a legal link in your main menu, so that's already one place taken care of.

When you add additional links to the footer, you're up to two places. Now, it's much more difficult for one of your readers to say that they couldn't find the information, especially when it's in two places on every single page.

The easiest way to handle the legal link is to make one link that goes to one page that links out to your documents. You can even make your own legal page that has a brief explanation of each of the documents, with a link at the end to read the full document.

When you organize the information this way, you only need to place one link in your footer that will take your

"Don't hide your legal documents. You have nothing to hide, so make them easy to find."

readers to all of your legal information at the very same time. From there, they simply need to pick the document they wish to read, and they'll have all the information they're looking for.

This also helps when it comes to keeping your blog legal. It's important under certain circumstances to have these different legal documents posted on your website.

While it's important to consult with your trade commission or a lawyer for the exact regulations, because they change, the more prominent you can make this placement, and the easier to find, the better.

Besides, if you're into blogging for the long-haul, then you really don't have anything to hide by telling your readers exactly what's in your privacy policy or your disclaimer.

If you don't want them to know what's going on, you are more than likely doing something that you shouldn't, and eventually that may become illegal.

Though I can't promise it, the vast majority of techniques and processes that feel slimy eventually become banned.

If they're not out right banned, they are restricted so heavily that they are no longer effective, so the end result is very similar.

It's much better to just be wide open about your legal documents as pertaining to your website, because the people that do care about it would like to know that you are not out to dupe them.

Link the Bottom

Reaching back to a previous idea, it may be beneficial for you to create one simple link at the bottom of your footer that takes the reader to the next step that you have determined to be where you want all of your traffic to go.

"A single link with a killer headline can take your readers exactly where you want them to go from the footer."

There are some good and bad things that can happen with this style of link, but depending on your blog, it may make sense for you.

Using a single link at the bottom of your footer has a couple of different advantages. First, it takes the reader to exactly the next place that you want them to go. Even if your readers would go someplace else given the choice, you get to send them exactly where you want instead.

This is good from the standpoint of trying to convert those readers into customers, because you can send them to one of your highest converting pages.

Another advantage is that you can give them the content that you want to give them. This can even be something like having them sign up to an email list so that way they never miss your next post. If you send your posts out regularly on an RSS email, then you'll be able to give them the next piece of content right when it comes out, just like you promised.

The downside of one simple link to take them to the next step is that a portion of your traffic is not going to click that link.

Additionally, the portion of traffic that doesn't click that link won't necessarily be because they don't like the call to action, it might simply be because they don't like that piece of content.

If you're sending them to another post, or a page, that call to action needs to be super effective when it comes to the text on that link.

You may even consider doing a graphic that links to your final destination. This way, you'll get to both visually and through

"The single call to action needs to be really well written to capture the most readers and get the click."

text communicate how awesome it would be for them to click on that particular piece of your blog.

If you're going to go with the one link strategy down at the bottom, you definitely need to do absolutely everything you can possibly think of in order to make that link as juicy, and as clickable as possible.

The more time you spend getting this right, the higher converting that particular piece will be.

On the other side of that link, it's important that you're hitting them with your absolute best stuff.

Even if you're going to a big sales page, the sales page still has to have a lot of value for the customer in order for it to make the most sense. You don't want to get a huge amount of conversions on a link, and then get no conversions on your sales page.

"The internet is an interesting place. Unless you try a lot of different things, you will never find out what works."

Don't be afraid to try some different things in the beginning when it comes to the one link strategy, because certain things are going to work better for certain people than others. The Internet is an interesting place, so unless you try different things, you'll never really find out what works and what doesn't.

Hide Something Fun

Finally, another strategy that you may want to consider is hiding something fun in your footer that the reader can find at the end. This needs to be something that you don't mention at all in your post, or something that you can tease very lightly for the people that will make it all the way to the end.

Maybe you have a really useful guide or download that is helpful for your readers. This can be a prime candidate for the footer, because it gives your reader a piece of content to take with them when they leave.

Your contact information will be inside of it of course, as well as a link to get back to the website whenever they need you.

Another fun thing might be a personal video that you create, thanking them for visiting your blog and helping them get to know you a little better.

If your reader has already made it to the bottom, and they like your style of writing, they might like getting to know you a little bit too.

This is where a video can be a fun thing to find, especially on a site that may not have a lot of video.

Tips and Tricks for Headers and Footers

Here are some tips and tricks to get your headers and footers set up for success:

- Keep your header short, informative, and as compact as possible so you don't eat up all of your above the fold area.

- The purpose of your header is just to reiterate that your reader clicked on the right thing when they left the search engine. Don't make it confusing.

- Your footer has a lot more flexibility than your header, because it's all the way down at the bottom of your post.

- While your header needs to remain pretty tight and businesslike, your footer can get a little over the top without causing any problems.

- Since the footer loads at the very end, make sure that you're giving your readers someplace to go, or something to click on when they get there.

- Consider adding multiple links to your best content, or simply adding one link to the piece of content that you want everyone to go to when they get to the end.

- Link to some of your freebies, or a fun piece of content that's a surprise for your reader. This is your last chance to hold onto them, so make it good.

Chapter Seven

Sidebars and Widgets

Your sidebar is the column on the right or the left of your blog, depending on the style, and the widgets are the different sections that you include in that sidebar. There are a few things to know about when it comes to sidebar design, and again simple is always the best choice.

Once you really get into blogging, you can spend more time working on your sidebar and making at the most effective. However, in the beginning you can have a pretty darn effective sidebar by going for a simple strategy and just sticking with it.

Like most sites, so much of your traffic is going to come from mobile that your sidebar is going to be more important for your desktop users.

Since the sidebar loads on the bottom of the content on a mobile device, most of the time it won't even be seen.

However, on desktop it's seen every time because it loads right along with the main content frame.

For the people that do see your side bar, it's important that you communicate effectively and that you share the resources you want them to stumble upon.

This way, even though it may not get the most eyes, your side bar will still be helpful to those that do see it.

Sidebars are Rarely Seen

Since mobile has taken over the majority of website sessions, the sidebar definitely doesn't have the same place of importance that used to have.

The experience of a website on mobile is drastically different than on desktop or tablet. Since phones are still small, at least when compared to tablets and computers, the content has to rearrange itself into one very tall vertical column.

"The experience of a website on mobile is drastically different than on a desktop."

When this happens, the theme has to make decisions on where to place everything. One of the decisions that is made is to place the sidebar immediately after the content, and before the footer.

Even though this might sound like you're not exposing your readers to your sidebar content, you still are, just in a little different way. While the content and desktop remains visible the majority of the time, you have to wait for all of the main ideas to pass by in order to show the sidebar on mobile.

This can actually be a good thing in disguise however, because if someone sticks with you all the way to the bottom, it shows that they like what you're sharing with them.

This means if you have some really good next steps that the person can take in your sidebar, you may have a higher chance of getting those clicks at the end.

Also, depending on what type of widgets you run in your side bar, and how long your content generally runs, your sidebar might only be visible for a few seconds on desktop too.

As you scroll down on the website, the sidebar and the main content move at the same speed. Once you get past the couple things that you'll have in your sidebar, they disappear at the top of your screen while you continue to scroll down the main column.

At this point, your sidebar might as will not even be there, and it was probably only seen for the first few seconds where the person was reading the top of the site.

In general, the behavior of people near the top of the website is different than the behavior of people near the bottom. Most people are kind of programmed to know that the beginning of the post is just fluff and introductions, so they tend to do a large jump scroll until they see something that resembles the meat of what they're looking for.

"In general, the behavior of people at the top of your website is different than the behavior at the bottom of your website."

If your side bar isn't very long, which is my recommendation, most of your desktop users will jump scroll right past it.

Again, this makes the sidebar much less visible than it used to be, and unfortunately it also makes it a lot less effective than it used to be when compared to the whole of your blog.

There are a couple ways to fix this problem though, and they'll be coming up later in the chapter. The sidebar can still be an effective part of your website, it's just only going to be effective for the people that see it.

Keep it Simple

Just like all good things, simple is generally the best choice. Simple designs, simple recipes, and simple pleasures are often the most profound. You can do so much better with a simple design crafted really well than trying to cram every single thing you can into your look.

When it comes to your sidebar, it's much better to just have a couple sections and make them super simple, but effective. This is way better than having too much going on, or creating a sidebar that can be confusing for your readers.

When you share too much with someone, they get overwhelmed.

"When you give your readers too many choices, they will choose the one you didn't give them, which is choosing noting."

This doesn't make it easier to make a decision, it makes it more difficult.

Even if there are technically less choices with only a couple of options, it's easier to get a person to choose out of two or three things than it is to get them to choose between 20 to 30.

Faced with so many choices, most people choose an option that isn't even in front of them, and that's the no option.

Remember, in every amount of choices you give your readers, there's always one additional choice, and that's to do nothing.

So if you have two links, your reader still has three choices.

In keeping your sidebar simple, you reduce the amount of choices that the reader has to make.

"If you have two links, your reader still has three choices."

That creates an environment where choosing something is much easier.

Fast Loading Sidebars

There are a lot of different widgets that you can choose to place in your sidebar. Some of these widgets are cleaner and simpler than others. Some of them are also a lot faster to load than others.

When it comes to your sidebar, this should be treated just like any other place on your website when it comes to loading speed.

The search engines have made it very clear that page speed is an important factor in the rankings. So, anything you can do to make your site load faster is a good choice.

As long as you're maintaining a good user experience, a fast loading website will help your search rankings, especially when compared to a similar site that doesn't load as quickly.

"In general, flashy widgets tend to consume more resources than text based static widgets."

Look at the different choices that you have for sidebar widgets. You may have to Google a few things, but in general you can pretty much tell by how sophisticated the widget looks whether it's a slow loader or not.

Image carousels, product sliders, and other heavy image based widgets eat up a lot more loading time than simple text based widgets.

Even though they look awesome, they are definitely going to take a longer time to get loaded up.

If you absolutely have to have some of these on your sidebar, do a speed test and make sure that they aren't bringing down your website.

Basically, you run the test with and without that particular widget activated, and see if there's a difference.

Likely there will be, and you can see if it's worth it or not.

Also, you may just want to open that version of the page in an incognito window so that way you can test the load time fresh and see how soon it becomes clickable for yourself.

Besides, with the sidebar not having quite as much prominence as it used to, image based content is probably better suited somewhere else.

Especially if it's something that you really want to

be seen, the sidebar may not be your best choice anyway.

Important Stuff on Top

Just like your website, the top of the sidebar should be used for important content that is a very small ask. This is the stuff that you want people to click on to get to know you better, and stuff that doesn't require anything other than a click in order to get the action you're looking for.

Especially on mobile, if you're lucky enough for the sidebar to even come into view, then it's important to get to the point right away, and open with your best material.

Your giving material is best placed here, and these posts will be the first interaction that your reader has with the sidebar section of the site.

Good candidates for the top of the sidebar include your highest performing content, newsletter sign-ups, and free downloads.

The content in the downloads will likely outperform your newsletter sign-up, unless there's an awesome reason to get on the list.

"Sometimes just promising someone exactly what they will get it better than giving them something in the hopes that they stick around."

This doesn't necessarily have to be a freebie, it can simply be the promise of great content delivered to them at a regular interval.

Sometimes, promising exactly what they'll get is much better than giving them something in hopes that they stick around. Most of the time they won't anyway.

Opening with your big stuff also maximizes the potential that you'll get your reader to take action.

Since the top of the sidebar is after your content, the original search term that brought the reader to your website has been satisfied. They probably already have the answer they came looking for, so at this point they're stumbling around essentially just looking in case they need something.

This is kind a like when you wander around the supermarket after you've gotten everything on your grocery list.

You don't necessarily know what you want, but you'll know you want it when you see it.

This is the same for your website. People down at the bottom are just making sure they've got everything they need before they leave.

If you can give them a good enough reason to stick around with your sidebar, they may click over and start the process again at the top of another blog post.

Use a Sticky Widget

One of the big problems with the sidebar on desktop is that it eventually disappears. The same thing happens on tablet. All that work, and all of that awesomeness, and it will likely be gone in just a few seconds.

There is a way to change that however, and it's called a sticky widget.

"The sticky widget is a huge opportunity for you."

Essentially, this is one of your widgets that doesn't go past the top of the screen as a user scrolls down.

All of the other widgets will disappear at the top, but this widget will hit the top of the container and stick there, no matter how long the reader scrolls.

This is a huge opportunity for you.

It's very rare that you get to hold an advertisement or a call action in front of a reader the entire time that they are viewing your site. A sticky widget does just that. It sticks at the top of the sidebar column the entire time the user is scrolling down to the main content. As they read, that widget sticks with them, as a constant reminder or call to get them to take another step.

"The deeper a person reads into your post, and the more they start to trust you, the more effective the call to action in your sticky widget becomes."

This type of widget is a good place to include one of your calls to action for selling a product or service.

As a customer reads further and further down your post, they start to develop that trust in you, and they might even start to like you. The deeper they go, the more effective that sticky widget becomes.

Even someone who is intently reading will naturally glance over at the different elements of a web page as they populate. This is partly out of awareness and partly out of the desire not to miss out on anything.

When they glance over and see that you've written a book, it may not do much for them in the beginning. However, the deeper they scroll, the more value that book may have in their mind.

Especially if you provide a very good experience for your reader, and you give them a lot of value, the deeper they go, the happier they will be. As they glance back at that sticky widget, suddenly your book becomes a much more powerful item than it was in the beginning.

At first, nobody's going to care that you've written a book. Why would they? They have no idea who you are, and they don't know if you have the answers for them.

It's only when they start reading your post, and they get pulled into your world that they finally begin to understand how great you are.

As you continue to show them the value that you can give, that sticky advertisement becomes almost magnetic. People that really like you will want to consume more of your material. When you use a sticky widget, you get to show that value piece and it sticks around for when the customer is ready to click.

"People are not going to go out of their way to buy from you."

That's probably the most beautiful part of a sticky widget. The widget just waits until the reader has had enough time to make a good decision, and then the call action is right there when they need it.

Believe it or not, there will be people that leave your website who would have purchased from you had a link been in the right place at the right time.

People are not going to go out of the way to buy things from you. You need to make it really easy and have your links available at the right time.

The problem with that is you have absolutely no

idea when the right time is. For some customers, it's closer to the beginning, for others the middle, and for others the end.

Rather than including a buy now button in every other sentence, the sticky widget does that for you in a much less obtrusive way.

No Meaningless Widgets

There is a huge temptation with new bloggers to jam every single widget you can get your hands on into your sidebar. After all, it's an easy win, and it adds some functionality to your website.

The problem is that it leads to information overload, and it makes your sidebar take longer to load.

Widgets are fun and exciting in the beginning, I totally get it. When you look at the amount of widgets that come stock in WordPress, you can create a sidebar that's a mile long. Then, when you look at all the different plug-ins that you can get, your sidebar and stretch around the world.

There is one big thing to think about when it comes to adding a widget to your sidebar, and it's a good filter to put every single one of them through before you decide to add them.

"None of this is for you, and none of this is to make you happy."

Ask yourself, is this benefiting my readers?

Everything that's on your site needs to be for your readers. None of this is for you, and none of this is to make you happy.

Widgets are fun, and they look neat, but unless they're really offering something of value for your readers, they are a complete waste of time for everyone.

Think about every widget, and make the decision to

do the right thing before you put anything on your website.

If you already have a sidebar that's loaded with a ton of widgets that you just picked out because they looked interesting, start cutting those back right away.

Especially in the case where you picked out a widget that you weren't even actively looking for, or you just stumbled upon, you really didn't need that one anyway.

"Get yourself down to the widgets that make the most sense and shoot for a compact sidebar right away."

Get yourself down to the widgets that make the most sense, and shoot for a compact sidebar that gets to the point right away.

Besides, if you're planning on using a sticky widget in that sidebar, it will have to be at the bottom, which means the more stuff you have in the way, the longer it will take to get to.

Let's say your average post length is 1000 words, and you have a sidebar that's about the same length as your post. In order for your sticky widget to be effective, people need to scroll down in order to get it into view.

When you sidebar is super long, it obviously takes a lot longer to get that sticky widget into place.

This means all of the awesomeness of that widget is going to be wasted as users scroll past a bunch of random widgets that really don't contribute to the success of your website at all.

It's even worse if your content is super short, or your sidebar is super long. You might even end up with a situation where your content disappears before your sidebar does, and that's definitely not a good user experience.

No Post Counters at First

Something to consider right away, especially as a beginning blogger is to make a decision on post counters and listing the amount of posts that you have on your site.

It's not about deceiving anyone, it's just not about advertising that you are brand new.

"Don't use a post counter in the beginning, especially when you are brand new."

The point of a post counter is to briefly show your readers how much amazing content is on your website. This can create a sense of value, because people really like a resource they can go to for a lot of information. If you have a brand new website, and you only have five posts, you can send the opposite signal.

It doesn't even matter if it's true. People tend to see a small number of posts on a site as a signal that it doesn't have a lot of information.

In contrast, your five posts could be the most information packed five posts about that particular keyword on the entire Internet, but it likely won't matter.

In the beginning, if you want to include a list of your categories, absolutely go ahead and do that.

However, what it asks you to toggle on or off the post counter feature, just leave that part off until you have enough posts that the numbers don't seem small.

This is one less widget that you don't have to worry about including in your sidebar, and that can help you keep that sidebar a little shorter, which will keep it more informative.

Only Use One Sidebar

As a general rule, you want to use only one side bar

on your website. There are some examples of websites that do OK with a sidebar on both ends, but this is the exception, not the norm.

Websites are made of columns. The side bar is a column. The main content is a column. Each of these columns takes up a certain amount of width, and if you put several columns together, there's only a certain amount of space to go around.

"Only use one sidebar on your site."

In a case like this, the size of the main column will have to adjust in order to fit the smaller amount of space on the screen, and that means you'll have skinnier content in general.

When you have one side bar, it generally represents about 20% to 35% of the total width of the screen on desktop. If you were to add another sidebar, you could end up taking half or more of the space.

This means your main content column will be very narrow and tall, which tends to not look very good on desktop.

You can experiment with this look of course, and make a decision based on the websites in your niche, and your particular needs.

However, most websites have a main content column with one sidebar that's either on the right or on the left. This is the format that most of your readers are comfortable with, and it can serve your blog well to look the same.

Mirror Successful Sites

Finally, when it comes to laying out your sidebars, it's a good idea to take a look at other successful blogs that are in your niche. This way, you'll get a sense of what your readers are used to seeing, and you can mirror those layouts on your own site.

It's not a matter of copying their content. It's a

matter of looking at the layout for tips and inspiration to help your own be more consistent with the expectation.

On certain sites, and in certain niches, things are supposed to be a certain way. While being disruptive is fun sometimes, it's also a good idea to provide a safe and trusted experience to people they come visit your site.

For example, if every website in your niche has no side bars, you may want to think about doing the exact same thing.

"While being disruptive is fun sometimes, it's also good to provide a safe and trusted user experience."

This way, when people come and visit your site, it doesn't have a totally different feeling than the sites they are used to visiting.

In the beginning, your readers will already be a little bit shy about being on your side instead of another.

It takes a little while to build up their comfort level, so everything you can do to make the experience comforting is a step in the right direction.

"Sometimes it's not about being inviting but it's more about not scaring people away when they arrive."

When you provide a look that's similarly laid out to other sites that have a higher level of trust than yours, you're helping provide an easy experience that doesn't scare people away on your site.

Sometimes it's not about inviting people as much as it is about not scaring them away once they get there. When you have a bizarre layout, or something that's completely inconsistent with everyone else in your space, it can be weird, and that scares people.

Look to the other sites in your niche, and see how they operate.

Pay attention to where they put their sidebars, how

many they use, and what type of elements are inside. Use these success clues to design your own sidebar, and you can be sure you have a similar experience when the user lands on your site.

It's beneficial to look at a few different sites and jot down some notes. For example, you can look at the top 10 sites in your genre and write down

"Once you see the common elements in other successful sidebars, you can so the same thing on your site."

how many side bars they use, where they're placed, and what number of widgets are present. Then, write down what those widgets are, and continue for all 10 sites.

When you get to the end, you'll notice a very clear trend. You may see right away that every site uses one side bar, they place it on the left, they include a search box at the top, followed by their greatest hits, and a sticky widget with a call to action.

Once you know the pattern, you can include the

same elements, in the same places, and put your own spin on them to match your site design.

At this point, your sidebars and widgets will be consistent with the rest of your space and the other players in your niche, and that will be comforting to your readers.

You'll get to put your own spin on them, but the nuts and bolts will be the same, and that's a good thing.

Tips and Tricks for Sidebars and Widgets

Here are some tips and tricks to make your side bars and widgets the best they possibly can be, and help your website be more effective:

- Side bars are hardly visible anymore, because most of the traffic ends up on mobile, and mobile places the side bar after your content.

- When designing your sidebar, only use a few widgets, and make them the most effective ones you can possibly pick.

- Get to the point right away at the top of your sidebar, especially since you may only have a short window when it shows up on mobile.

- Use a sticky widget to help yourself, because it will always be there just waiting for the moment when your customer is finally ready to buy.

- Simple side bars, with simple widgets are a much better choice than anything overly exotic, elaborate, or that takes forever to load.

- The sidebar is not for entertainment, that's the job of your main content.

Chapter Eight

Evaluating the Post

Once your post is written, the editing phase begins. It's important that while you're writing, you don't do very much editing.

"Writing and editing come from two different places in your brain."

These skills come from two different spots in your mind, and it's best to get the words out of your brain before you go back and make your edits.

Once you do start editing, it's good to have a strategy to be able to edit for content, grammar, and anything else that might slow down your reader. This is your opportunity to really polish your post, and that will help your audience enjoy the content even more.

It's important that you do a thorough job editing your work, and that you do everything you can to catch the different mistakes that need to be fixed.

Don't let it paralyze your process of course, because you can technically edit and tweak forever if you don't stop yourself. However, all you really need to do is spend enough time that you correct the overwhelming majority of your mistakes and your post will do just fine.

Coming up I'll show you several ways that you can make the editing process easier, and this will help you create a blog post that people love.

Editing in general isn't as fun as creating, but with

the right strategies, you can minimize the time and maximize the effect.

Edit in the End

Whatever you do, it's important that you save all of your edits to the very end of the process. Writing and editing are two completely different things, and they come from two completely different places in your brain.

"When you switch between writing and editing, it's like switching between forward and reverse in a car."

Writing is the creative side while editing is the analytical side.

When you switch back-and-forth between writing and editing, it's almost like switching between forward and reverse in a car.

You have to bring the car to a complete stop to

switch directions, then, you have to bring it to a complete stop again to start going to the original way.

This is a lot of back-and-forth with a lot of stops in between. It's also very jarring on your mind, and it robs you of the ability to get into the flow state when it comes to your writing.

The flow state is where the words are just coming to you effortlessly, and you feel almost like you can't say or type the wrong thing. It's a wonderful experience, and it only shows up when you remove the editing barrier.

That being said, if you ever want to have almost divine like clarity and an inspirational writing experience, you have to allow yourself the ability to just express the words and not worry about editing them.

When you do this, you'll enter that flow state a lot more often, and that can sometimes be the difference between an average writing session and a few thousand extra words in that writing session.

There have been many times while writing when I've felt very comfortable, and the words just came to me effortlessly.

In this state, I've been able to write over 5000 words an hour for a few hours without stopping. It's an amazing feeling, and you can lay down a ton of excellent work in a very short amount of time.

"In the flow state, I've been able to write over 5,000 words an hour for a few hours without stopping."

This is also with dictation of course, but as long as the words hit the paper, it doesn't matter how they get there.

On your next writing project, make it a point to do all the writing from beginning to end without editing a single word. This means unless you completely change the sentence that you're currently working on, because you started it incorrectly, you don't correct a single thing.

Even the smallest of edits need to wait. Don't worry about capital letters, commas, or anything else.

At the very end of the document is the only time you can go back and read over your work and complete all of your edits.

If you start writing like this, you'll be extraordinarily happy with the way that you're able to create a large volume of material in a short amount of time. It's not crappy material either, it's just a rough draft ready to be edited and polished to final form.

Write first, and edit last. You'll be glad that you got this little technique worked into your process.

Errors Slow Your Readers

One of the biggest reasons to edit your work is that errors and mistakes slow down your readers, and they cause confusion.

"All of the magic goes away when people discover an error in your post."

Anyone that has read a book and found a spelling mistake knows exactly what I'm talking about. I'm sure you've been there before, where suddenly you're stopped dead in the middle of what's going on and you notice you've discovered a mistake.

All of the magic in that post, or the lesson to be learned, or anything else that the author was claiming to teach is now completely out the window.

You are totally fixated on that error, even though it's really very basic and it doesn't mean the author is an idiot.

This is a distraction, and it's something that you want to try to avoid as much as possible in your own writing. The last thing you want to do right in the middle of your amazing blog post is get people thinking about something else.

When they find a spelling mistake, or severe grammatical error, a lot of people will stop, and that's no good.

Obviously you want to cater to your audience, and you also want to be sure that the average person can read your material.

However, there's a big difference between using poor grammar because you don't know it and using simple language. Simple language is still grammatically correct. Mistakes are mistakes, and simple and simple.

It's easier to impress your audience with simple language written well, and it's better than complex language with lots of mistakes.

Most of your spelling mistakes aren't really going to be problems, because the computer will catch most of them. Spend your time looking for words that look the same but aren't quite the same, that's where your biggest opportunity is.

Go over your post really well, and don't give the readers anything to distract them from its awesomeness.

Too Many Errors Make You Look Bad

When it comes to blogging, or writing for websites in general, I do believe that there is an acceptable amount of errors that won't be distracting.

"There is an acceptable amount of errors that is not distracting to your readers."

No matter how good you are at editing you're always going to miss a few things. This is normal, and I don't want you to think that you have to catch every last mistake before you're allowed to hit the publish button.

It's not expected that you catch absolutely everything. However, it is expected that you catch the vast majority of things.

Anything above a couple minor errors is frowned upon, and it starts to make it look unprofessional.

Worse than that, depending on how many grammatical errors you make, or even word choice errors, you can make the language look as if it wasn't written by a native speaker.

While there is nothing wrong with writing in a different language than you are comfortable with, you don't want it to appear obvious that you're struggling with the words.

This can make it difficult for some newer writers.

However, it's well worth the effort to sound as fluent

as you possibly can when you write your posts.

When you make lots of errors, you can also run the risk of people associating your mistakes with your intelligence level, and subsequently your ability to teach on your blog.

"People will associate lots of mistakes with a low intelligence level, and then they will start to question whether you are qualified to teach them."

After all, every blog post is teaching people something, and you need to have some level of credibility and authority in order for people to accept you as a good teacher.

When your grasp of the language is less than acceptable, it starts to develop thoughts about your overall education level when it comes to the subject you're dealing with.

Unless you're very good at delivering that subject matter, the language difficulties can overshadow your good content.

If this happens, you could end up losing readers even though your information is good.

Spend the time to go through your posts and you won't really have to worry about committing a very large amount of errors. You also will likely not have to worry about committing so many that you cause your readers to doubt your credibility. That's the bigger issue that you definitely want to avoid.

Another thing that errors can do is cause issues for you in the search engines. The search algorithms are

"Search engine algorithms are based on language, so your spelling is important."

based on language, so if you are misspelling words or phrases, they aren't going to match the search terms that the different search sites think you are targeting.

This means unless the reader also makes the same

spelling mistake, you might not get any traffic for that search term at all.

This is also not a good outcome because the more traffic you can get from the search engines the better. This is completely free traffic that simply has to do with the way you write your posts. It's all about the keywords and phrases, and simply typing the right words in the right order can be the difference between your post being found or not.

When you add misspellings and improper English or grammar, you compound the issue even more.

Check the Post on Desktop

The first thing you should do with your post after it's written is do your edits on your desktop computer. This is most likely the place where you do with the majority of your writing in WordPress, so this is the easy first place to start.

Scroll back to the top of your post and start reading. This is the most basic way to edit your material.

All you need to do is read it from start to finish, and pay attention to a few different things that come up along the way. As they do, you'll be able to make changes, fix your work, and apply the final polish before you're ready to schedule the post to go live.

So what are you looking for? Above all else the most important thing you're looking for is making the post easy to read. When you read your work, check that it flows easily, and that there are no difficult sections to read through. If you get stuck on a sentence and you

"As you edit your post, think about making it easy to read."

have to read it more than once, it's probably a good idea to try and adjust that sentence to be more understandable.

Your writing should move from sentence to sentence and paragraph to paragraph effortlessly.

As you read, it should feel natural, and not difficult. If you find sections that are a little too dense, or sentences that are a little too long, go ahead and break up those areas to make them easier to understand.

As you read through, you'll also notice mistakes in word choice, spelling errors, and spots that just don't make sense.

Fix these as you come to them, and by the time you get to the end of your blog post, you should have something that reads pretty darn well at that point.

"Fix errors as you come to them, and by the time you reach the end your post should look pretty good."

It's also a good idea to pay attention to formatting as you are reading through and editing.

Look at the way your images are placed on your post, and make sure they are set correctly. Ensure that the text drops around the bottom of your images appropriately so that way you don't cause any funny formatting issues when the post goes live.

A little trick that can help, especially with wide screen computer monitors, is to format the size of the window in WordPress to be about the same size as the final site will be when it goes live.

This won't make a lot of difference if you are using a much larger font, but what it can do is help avoid mistakenly thinking that the content will really be as wide as it looks in WordPress.

Something that you'll notice when you do a live preview of your post is that it's going to look much different live than it does in the WordPress editor.

This is one aspect that I do wish could be controlled a little bit better, but until that comes around, make sure you check the live preview when it comes to formatting and placing your images appropriately.

If you have to read through your post a couple times on desktop in order to make sure that you caught everything, don't feel bad about it.

Spending a little extra time on editing doesn't hurt, especially in the beginning. Over time, you'll get much better at laying down the right words the first time, and you'll also get better at catching more of your edits on the very first round.

Remember, if it's awkward for you to read, your readers will definitely have a hard time.

"If it's awkward for you to read, it will definitely be hard for your reader to understand."

After all, they didn't write it, and they don't fully understand it.

With that in mind, any time you encounter a section of your text that's a little awkward, or feels like it slows you down, consider working on that section to make it easier to read.

Not only will this improve your writing, it will improve the readability of your posts, and make them easier to understand.

Check the Post on Mobile

After checking out your post on Desktop, it's time to take a look at the massive transformation of your post on mobile.

When your post is read on the phone, it's going to look much different than it looks on desktop. Most posts look great on desktop, but then end up completely reformatting when they go to mobile.

It's important to look at the way your post resolves on the phone in order to address any issues that are not easy to detect looking at the desktop version.

The majority of these issues are going to be formatting versus editing.

Since everything turns into a very tall and narrow column on mobile, the biggest thing to look for is the size of your paragraphs.

A paragraph that might look medium length on desktop can look downright intimidating on mobile. This is where you can turn off your readers because they see a huge block of text and they run away.

Since the majority of your readers are going to be using their phones, it's important to break up these paragraphs even farther. The desktop look isn't going to change very much, it will just look a little bit looser. That's OK though, because even people working on a desktop appreciate being able to build up some momentum and some scrolling speed as they work through the content.

"The biggest thing to look for on mobile is the size of your paragraphs."

Make a note of any sections that appear too long on a mobile phone, and go back to those sections to break them down into smaller chunks. This will make a big difference in how fast your readers leave your page, and it will also help them skip a lot less of your content.

When readers encounter an intimidating section of a post, they either leave or they skip it. A few will actually read it, most of them will leave or skip. Unfortunately, most of them leave.

"If you can't the entire image on the screen at once, it's too tall."

Beyond the paragraphs, make sure that your headings look detailed enough that they stick out, and that your bullets or numbered lists resolve correctly too.

If you have any images are too tall, it's a good idea to go back and shave those down as well. As a general rule, if you can't see the entire image on the screen at once, it needs to be shorter.

Once you're done with all of your mobile checks,

there's only one last place to go.

Check the Post on Tablet

Most tablets have a fairly similar look and feel to the desktop. It's still a condensed version, so the column becomes narrower and taller.

Though definitely not as narrow and tall as mobile, there can be some formatting issues that pop up on a tablet that don't pop up on the other two.

Go through the post much the same way as you did on desktop and mobile. Look for formatting errors, sections that don't quite resolve right, and if you catch some spelling or writing mistakes, go ahead and correct those too.

Even though the mobile and tablet are more for formatting, you can still use this as an exercise in editing the words too.

Once you're satisfied that the post looks right on all three devices, then you can be confident in scheduling it for publishing knowing that your work will look professional, and that it won't make your readers wonder if you're qualified to teach them.

Read the Post Out Loud

Editing can be a little bit tricky, especially when you have to edit your own work. Our brains are beautiful and wonderful organs, and in the interest of making things easier, your brain will often switch out words and clean up sentences that you've written in order to help them make sense to you.

> *"Your brain will fix errors and switch out words as you read your own writing."*

While this is a mini miracle, it's terrible for the editing process.

The problem with reading and editing your own work is that you just wrote your own work. You have a certain way that you like to write sentences, and your brain knows that.

On top of that, your brain will fix little mistakes and make your work actually sound better to you than it does in real life.

If someone else were to read it, they would notice different things, and have a different experience than you do.

One of the ways to counteract this problem is to read your work out loud.

"The problem with editing your own work is that you wrote your own work."

Read it out loud, slowly, and listen to the words you are saying.

This isn't an exercise where the goal is to get to the end of the post. The goal is to hear all the words and catch all of the mistakes so you can fix them.

If you just read through your post out loud, super quickly, you might as well not do this exercise at all.

Your goal is to fix the words and make them flow in a way that keeps your reader engaged with the post. Read the words out loud, slowly, and you'll hear things that just don't quite sound right.

When you do, address them right away, and then continue working through the rest of the post.

It's a little difficult to understand at first, but you want to focus on what you're hearing as you are reading your post out loud. You are going to be combining three different things at once. Reading, speaking, and listening.

Even though all three of these things are going on simultaneously, the one you care the most about is the listening. Listen to the way the words sound, and hear them coming out of your mouth. When you put your attention in this area, and you read at a slightly slower than normal speed, you'll catch a lot more mistakes than reading in your head.

Have a Friend/Spouse Read the Post

Another strategy that works really well for editing your work and actually catching everything is to have a friend or spouse read your post. This can be anyone that you know and trust.

"The best part of having someone else edit your post is that they are not you."

The benefit of having someone other than you read your material and check for mistakes is simply that the person isn't you.

They don't organize their sentences the same way that you do, so their mind won't fix your mistakes automatically.

They also read from a users perspective, so they will be more qualified to point out things that don't make sense.

It's even better if the person doing the reading has a mild interest in the subject matter that you are covering. This way, they are even closer to what the end-user is going to experience, and they can also provide feedback on the information.

In reality, you'll be extremely lucky to find someone that enjoys the same content, has a healthy interest in the subject, and is willing to edit for grammar, spelling, content, and information.

That's a pretty tall order.

Instead, if you can find someone that will simply read it through and help you point out areas that are a little awkward, or where you chose the wrong word, that would be plenty.

In a case like this, you may be able to rely on your

spouse to help you get through your posts for one final edit before get them ready to publish.

Another thing you might be able to do is arrange to swap posts with another blogger. This way, you can help them edit their material, and they can help you edit yours.

Work out a deal between the two of you for the amount of material of course, and together you can help each other become more polished bloggers.

When you read the other blogger's work, you are much better suited to catch their mistakes. The same thing goes for when someone else reads yours.

They are going to find things that you never even thought about, and they will notice things that sailed right past you. That's just the nature of editing your own work versus editing the work of another writer.

If you have the ability to get someone else to help

you, and they are reliable, that's definitely a relationship that you want to take care of.

Offer Rewards for Catching Mistakes

A fun way of catching your mistakes involves using your readers to help you in the process. You can offer a bounty or reward on your website for every mistake that a reader catches.

This doesn't have to be monetary in nature, it just needs to be something that makes the reader feel good.

"Try offering a reward to your readers for catching mistakes and reporting them."

Depending on your niche, there are a lot of different ways to reward your readers without even having to spend any money.

For example, if you are teaching people how to

write, you might offer to link to one of their short stories or some other piece of content they've created.

A link from your website to another can be a very good thing, and it can help that reader get a little bit more exposure for their work.

You might also give them a shout out on social media and tag their profile with a thank you message for helping you become a better writer.

This ends up getting the helper more exposure, and possibly even some traffic from the social shares.

If you sell a product, you can offer a discount.

In the end, a discount is sometimes what you need in order to get someone to buy anyway, so even giving 10% off when someone finds a mistake can turn someone who had no intention of buying something into a customer.

Don't let that sound selfish. As long as your

products are good, and they serve your customers, helping them make the decision to buy is still better for them than it is for you.

Even if you don't offer rewards, sometimes all you need to do is send out a really honest thank you email when someone catches a mistake, and they will continue to do the same thing for you in the future.

Most readers are nice enough people, and if they like you, they will like helping you too.

Any time someone sends you a mistake, fix it right away, and then write them at least a paragraph or two thanking them for their help. Small mistakes do add up, and this person definitely didn't need to take any time to tell you about what happened. Since

"When your product is good, helping your readers make the decision to buy is always more in their interest than yours."

they went out of their way to make you better, go

out of your way and make sure they are thoroughly thanked.

Address Site Speed Early

Finally, while this doesn't have to do with editing your work exactly, it does have to do with how your post works in general.

It's important to pay attention to your site speed early in your blogging adventure. The more you pay attention to this now, the less heartbreak you'll have in the future.

"Don't fall in love with any themes or plugins that ruin your site speed."

The reason it's important now is so you don't fall in love with any themes or plug-ins that are severely detrimental to the speed of your site.

Slow websites do not get the same traffic as fast websites, and the search engines prioritize speed over many other factors. In fact, if you have a website with good content and killer speed, you can actually do better than some websites whose content is a little better, but their speed is significantly worse.

Before you install a plug-in or a theme on your site, one of the first things you need to do is a little searching to see how it will affect your site.

"If you find your plugin on the naughty list, don't use it."

Especially for the plug-ins that are rated as being very slow, this information is extraordinarily easy to find. If you have a theme or a plug-in that's on the naughty list, then it really doesn't matter how awesome it looks.

Choosing speed, you need to keep looking for something else that isn't going to slow down your site.

For most WordPress sites, the biggest offenders are your plug-ins.

These are little aftermarket additions to your website that you can download for free, or you can pay for in some cases. These are written by anyone, and there is definitely a big difference between the good ones and the bad ones.

Research all of your plug-ins thoroughly, and even if you have to lose a tiny bit of functionality, choose the plug-in that's the fastest.

If you can do without it, don't use the plug-in at all.

The fastest plug-in is the one you don't install, and you definitely don't want to sacrifice a lot of speed for a little bit of convenience.

> *"The fastest plugin is the one you don't install."*

There are a lot of different programs that you can use to test your site speed, and it's important to do these tests regularly so that way you have a good understanding of where your side lands on the speed scale. Most of these are free, but some of them are paid, and it's your choice which way you go.

However, since Google is the king of search, I recommend using their speed testing tool.

When it comes to how fast Google thinks your website is, they aren't using a third-party tool to figure that out. They are using their own tool.

For that same reason, you need to use their tools in order to determine your own site speed. It's a fairly easy process, and all you need to do is plug in your website address and it will tell you where you are good, and where you need to improve.

Just a heads up, this can be overwhelming at first. Most of these programs will return a list of things to fix that look like they are written in a foreign language.

There is a lot to digest, and in the beginning it can seem like it's all impossible to understand.

Don't let yourself become worried by what you see.

Just take a look at some of the biggest offenders, and start Googling how to fix them. You might also be able to call your host on a couple of occasions, as it's likely that they are involved with some of the problems anyway.

"Search how to fix the problems that the speed checker reports, and then start fixing them."

Attack them one at a time, and eventually you'll understand the majority of the suggestions that you're reading.

Keep your speed in check from day one, and you won't have to go back and do any massive overhaul to fix the problem down the road.

It's much easier to change themes or update an

entire website when it only has a couple dozen pages. Once you have a couple thousand, that's a whole different game.

Tips and Tricks for Evaluating the Post

Here are some tips and tricks for evaluating your post that can help you ensure that you are delivering the most polished content possible every single time:

- Edit your work on desktop, tablet, and mobile. You need to address all three in order to have the best user experience.

- Pay the most attention to ease of reading, and flow. It's important that your words and sentences are easy to read, and string together in a logical manner.

- If you have the luxury of getting someone else to help edit your work, it can be really beneficial to point out sections that you just don't notice, because you wrote it yourself.

- Address your side speed early, and don't fall in love with any themes or plug-ins that will weigh your site down.

Afterword

Now you have everything you need to create a great looking blog post, perfectly formatted for your readers. The answers will be easy to find, your content will be organized, and your users will be happy to start building trust with you.

These little things all make a big difference together, and though they may not seem like much, simple changes that make it easier to read your posts do make a huge difference in the end.

As you continue to use these different strategies in

your posts, always remember that your number one job as a blogger is to give the best answer to the question that your post is meant to solve, and make it easy to find.

If you keep these two things in mind, it will help you a lot as you develop your blog.

Happy Writing.

Disclaimer

This book is meant for educational purposes, and to help new bloggers format their content.

Any claims in this book about results are merely motivational in nature, and are not intended to be an indication that you will actually achieve the same results.

The thing about blogging is that you really need to work at it for a long time. It's not a fast thing, or a quick fix. It requires a lot of work, and no one book can give you the answers.

Since so much work needs to be done, and so much patience is required to be successful, most people end up failing and quitting long before they see any revenue.

That's the honest truth. Most of you will fail long before you see any money simply because you won't have the determination to stick with it long enough.

I can't tell you that this book will make you successful, I can only tell you that following the guidelines will help you format and write your posts in an easier to read manner.

That can help you become a better blogger, but you will need to do a lot more work in order to make money.

If you are not into this for the long haul, then I don't recommend blogging. You really need to have the focus to go for years without seeing results sometimes in order to finally get somewhere, and even that is not guaranteed.

I wish you the best with everything I teach in this book, but in the end the results are completely up to you.

Only you can be all the things that are needed to be successful, and though I hope my book can be a part of that, it won't make your blog an overnight success.

This book will only be one small part of an amazing journey of learning, mistakes, breakthroughs, setbacks, and leaps forward. It's one piece in a puzzle, and without the others, you can never see the full picture.

Keep learning, keep pushing, and when you get close to quitting, remember why you started. If you can do that long enough, and keep going when everything says to quit, you might be fortunate enough one day to actually make a little money blogging.

Happy writing.

Contact Me

If you have any questions about what you have read, please reach out and I will be glad to help.

You can email me at:
info@letsmakeablog.com

You can also send paper mail to:
Brian Forbes
22424 S Ellsworth Loop Road Suite 1967
Queen Creek, Arizona 85142

I will be glad to help you, and I look forward to the opportunity.

Happy Writing!